The Illusion of Achievement

The Illusion of Achievement

How the Public Moves and What Motivates Them

Ahmed Hassan Moshrif

Translated by Haya N Thabet

THE ILLUSION OF ACHIEVEMENT
Ahmed Hassan Moshrif

Published by Nomad Publishing in 2023
Email: info@nomad-publishing.com
www.nomad-publishing.com
Cover design: Lucie Wimetz

ISBN 9781914325847

© Ahmed Hassan Moshrif 2023

 The Publishers would like to thank the Harf Literary Agency

Disclaimer: The content and any opinions included in such content reflect the views and opinions of the author and do not reflect the opinions and beliefs of the publisher, the translator, Tarjim program, or any of their affiliates. The author is solely responsible for any statements made in such content and any translation is made based on the perception of the author from the original language or source of information prior to any translation or adaptation made.

Contents

Foreword	15

PART ONE: STATUS
INSTANT HAPPINESS 21

Instant happiness following depression	23
Instant Happiness and Human Evolution	27
Procrastination and the Instant	
Happiness Monkey	33
Public Status	37
The Ego and the Idea	41
Reading the logic of the Public	43
Social status	47
The owner of a luxury wallet, the doctor and the	
vegetable merchant	49
About Appearances and Initial Impressions	55

A REFLECTION ON STATUS AND
MATERIALISM 57

Why you should distance yourself from school	
friends?	57
Hatoon Kadi and Social Status	61
In front of Harrods department store	65
The search for social status	
and the attempt to prove it is inherited	
from our ancestors	71
Talking about social status is easy	81
The most important matter is the existing	

social status	83
The pursuit of social status (through borrowing)	85
Seeking social status without investing oneself in a specialization	89
The problem with some positive people	91
Why is it that what we lack owns us?	93
Why do I have this desire to stop reading Arabic books?	97

PART TWO: THE REWARD
THE REWARD AND HUMANITY 103

The Desire for Rewards	105
Emails	107
WhatsApp	109
The attempt to refrain from receiving messages	111
Analysis of attempts to resolve the issue	115
Twitter	117
Reward means reciprocation	119
The Collective Mind	121
The Story of the Land	127
Real Work in people	131
Breaking the fast for a wealthy person	133
The employee's sense of achievement and the accomplished employee (after leaving a job)	137

PART 3: THE IMPACT
THE EGO AND LEAVING AN IMPACT 143

Success and Leaving an impact	147
Examples of Leaving an Impact	149
Our Lives and Leaving an impact	151

LEAVING AN IMPACT THROUGH WORK — 153

- Carl Jung and Deep Work — 157
- The problem of the economy and modern society — 161
- Quick gains — 163
- Woody Allen — 167

ART AND DEEP WORK — 169

- Humanity and Great Minds with Hani Naqshabandi — 169
- Our Other Version of Deep Work — 173
- An Ordinary Story — 177
- The artistic human — 181
- Working with creativity — 183
- Achievement is an Accumulative Process — 185

A READING BETWEEN CREATIVITY AND REPETITION — 187

- What is creative work? — 187
- Creative Work vs. Repetition or Memorization — 189
- Why Don't Our Minds Work as We Want Them To? — 191
- Where is the Link between creativity and deep work? — 193

PART 4: IMPLEMENTATION
THE EQUATION OF EFFORT VERSUS TIME — 197

- Where does the illusion of achievement fit here? — 201
- Identifying where time and effort are spent — 203
- Minimization, Not Addition — 205

Steve Jobs and minimalism	209
The Things That Don't Change	213

PRODUCTIVITY AND DEEP WORK — 215

The To-Do List and the Difference Between an Option and a Choice	215
Tom Ford	219
Don't Break the Chain	221

THE RELATIONSHIP BETWEEN WORDS AND TAKING ACTION — 223

Working on My Next Novel	225
Comparing ourselves to others	227

DEEP WORK AND EXTENDED TIME — 231

Amr Diab	233
Richard Feynman	241
Neal Stephenson	243
Finale	249
Selected Readings & Bibliography	255

Dedication…

*Arena Moshrif,
All beauty comes from you, and all love is for you*

*Haitham AlRahbi,
The inspiration came from you and the real achievement was in knowing you, my friend*

*Abdullah Kotbi,
You engaged, you wrote, you cared, as if caring was your life's purpose*

"The masses have never thirsted after truth. They turn aside from evidence that is not to their taste, preferring to deify error, if error seduce them. Whoever can supply them with illusions is easily their master; whoever attempts to destroy their illusions is always their victim. An individual in a crowd is a grain of sand amid other grains of sand, which the wind stirs up at will."

Gustave Le Bon
French polymath, 1841–1931

"Whenever you find yourself on the side of the majority, it is time to pause and reflect."

Mark Twain
American writer, humourist and essayist, 1835_1920

Foreword

Human nature drives us to pursue ever greater gains without exerting much effort. It can start with parking the car in a wrong spot to save time and end with catastrophic losses in the stock market while attempting to make a quick profit without having to work for it.

As beginners, we writers often fall in love with our work and imagine the book is in our hands even before we have finished writing it. At the same time, we also struggle with the idea of sitting down every day for seemingly long hours to write.

Similarly, the painter loves "what has been drawn" yet challenges herself at every waking moment to get up and draw, immediately.

With all such situations, the feeling of accomplishment in our lives remains wonderful.

And here I say "feeling" of accomplishment, not the accomplishment itself. That is another subject we will delve into in greater detail.

Consider this: who among us does not desire to be accomplished in life?

It is certain that there is no person holding this book and reading this sentence right now who does not want to accomplish something in life

Nevertheless, a more important question arises here. Are most of us preoccupied with accomplishment or with trying to experience the feeling of accomplishment?

The feeling of accomplishment is rather "the illusion of accomplishment" and the actual accomplishment is the "real work."

Many feelings of accomplishment are possible without experiencing actual achievements that bring about real and tangible change. Most people strive for the feeling rather than the work, and the problem arises when we confuse the actual work with the feeling that we have worked.

Questions about this concept revolved in my mind daily until I posited an acceptable delineation of it in this book, where I present the difference between the illusion of accomplishment and real work in the collective mind, or what is called "the public perception".

I hope the reader does not understand from these words that I have positioned myself among the accomplished. What matters is that I have tried to present this idea so I could write about it, directing my thoughts to myself before transferring them in words to others. If I were indeed one of the truly accomplished, my presence would have been felt by different spectra of society and all the people around me, without exception, would have evolved to become better human beings.

In any case, this book is an attempt to bring the idea to the table and I hope it comes to fruition.

The other matter is: how do most people embark on this path?

There are many considerations that drive the individual to engage with others throughout their day and even their life.

A famous personality, on Snapchat for example, can feel wonderful when her followers interact with her, yet she may abandon the enterprise if after a few attempts no one pays her any attention. However, in the reverse case the feelings of her followers are activated once they allocate time to follow the celebrity's lead. They have an opportunity that did not exist years ago, to see a beautiful girl from their environment appearing to them every day, where they gain information from her (on the fly) along with all kinds of suggestions for new restaurants and places to see and visit. Other followers may simply be satisfied with entertaining themselves instead of committing to watching a movie or series on television, or investing time in reading a book.

The world is changing and entertainment channels are evolving.

What keeps the famous personality going is the interaction of others (the public). No matter how much it increases, we cannot consider her continuous appearance (in this case on Snapchat) a real accomplishment that adds value to society. All she does is keep appearing, with frequent and regular greetings on her followers' screens while sharing with them what she does during her day.

If we were to put things in their proper perspective, we would find many personalities suddenly emerged to vent their lives in the media, only to quietly disappear without anyone noticing them missing. It is possible, if rare, for the opposite to happen. Social media influencers appear and create substantial social change in their surroundings.

Only then can we call what they have done real work.

Leo Tolstoy's novel "War and Peace" is a real work that remained present for more than a hundred years after his death.

Establishing major companies is real work.

The creation of paintings, even if they don't get exhibited at famous galleries, can be called real work.

The late Dr. Abdulrahman AlSumait's philanthropic activities are also real work.
Writing an article is real work.
Directing a film is real work.
Striving to serve other people's needs is real work.
Continuing to learn new things is real work.

This book is a research project that includes my opinions and perspectives that stemmed from a process of internal questioning, from within myself, which is where these viewpoints were first birthed, then formed, then evolved, and finally documented. They all revolve around the following points:
1. Why do we obsess with sharing pictures of ourselves on social media channels, and how does this affect our lives?
2. Why do we care more about others' opinions of us than our opinions of ourselves?
3. Why do we strive so hard for prestigious social status, and why do we seek to buy things beyond our financial capabilities?
4. Why do we share so many preachy messages on social media channels?
5. What is the difference between real work and what we think is real work?
6. What does it mean to leave an impact, and why should we care about leaving an impact?

The first two parts of the book discuss the details of my issue, and the last two parts present solutions for them.
Enjoy reading,
Ahmad

PART ONE: STATUS

INSTANT HAPPINESS

Instant happiness is the desire to experience pleasure or psychological gratification without delay or postponement. In other words, when you want to feel pleasure, you want it right now, you want it immediately.

Instant happiness drives about ninety percent of our daily actions subconsciously, without necessarily considering their consequences or their impact on others. This often leads many of us, myself included, to overlook the harmful effects of certain daily habits, such as consuming excessive sugar, lack of regular exercise, not realizing the dangers of sleep deprivation, wasting time in the early morning hours on trivial matters, and spending excessive time on mobile phones or television screens throughout the day.

The time spent on social media platforms following the lives of others is often not considered a waste of time but rather a primary source of entertainment. A dilemma arises when one's interactions with others on social media exceed normal limits or when one's accomplishments are solely defined by their social media presence. In such cases, individuals find themselves depleting a significant amount of time and mental effort on matters that may not serve their long-term goals.

I attended a reading club meeting with a group of young people under the age of twenty to discuss a book. I concluded the meeting with a question, aiming to encourage them to spend more time reading books over the weekends. The question was:

"How do you spend most of your time during the weekend?"

One of the most conscious among the youth group answered:

"On our phones, most of the day. There's nothing more entertaining and easier than spending a lot of time on social media platforms and watching YouTube videos. If we decide to go out both days over the weekend, it would require permission from our parents and incur unnecessary expense."

What the young person said applies to various age groups. The easiest and least expensive way to combat boredom is to spend more time on social media platforms, to the extent that some individuals appear content with merely observing the lives of others.

Instant happiness following depression

Feeling bored or distressed? No problem. Take a picture of yourself and post it.

Smile for that picture of yourself while telling others that you are fine. If your level of depression increases slightly, let it be known with a non-smiling picture that you feel bored or distressed. It only takes a few moments for someone to comment or interact with you and a part of the distress quickly disappears.

Notice here that I have talked about a specific and temporary condition, which is distress.

Afterwards, I discussed the self-deception of feeling well without ever addressing the actual cause of the distress. Such behaviour triggers a well-known addictive state due to the rise in dopamine levels, the "happiness hormone," which is generated and increased unnaturally by various types of addictive substances, including engagement with social media platforms.

Social media platforms have become both our refuge and tranquilizer in life. While they are already the easiest source of entertainment, they have also become the easiest superficial remedy for distress and depression. I fear they are also the main motivator in deceiving ourselves with daily accomplishments that are not truly achievements but rather a feeling of accomplishment.

The discerning reader knows that universal law tells us

what comes quickly also goes quickly. This may include the localized remedies of social media, leaving the root of the problem and its cause untouched. It's similar to a patient who takes a lot of painkillers and tranquilizers while neglecting the correct treatment for the illness. Despite that, they still have the option to spend effort and money on painkillers instead of investing them in effective therapeutic approaches.

In this context, we ask a straightforward question: If we compare the scattered and time-consuming social media over the past week with the number of hours that could have been invested in achieving a long-term goal (such as writing a novel, working on a delayed project, or reading books that have been sitting on the shelf for a year), would we discover a vast difference between the two ways of spending time? Clearly, the answer is yes.

The other question is: Why, if we can answer this question, can't we proceed to find a solution and implement it? The answer is simply because the solution does not involve immediate happiness, and long-term projects require time and effort, with no guarantee of short-term results.

We may discover halfway through that the book is very boring, or we feel a bit lost in the project we are working on. Consequently, our minds turn to compensating for this time and effort by engaging in quick activities that positively affect our psyche. There is nothing more delightful than a luxury meal full of carbohydrates in the midst of a project or receiving comments on a picture we post on social media, as we wait for someone to comment or praise us. The greater challenge here is not to surrender to such instincts. We can instead resist the temptation to immerse ourselves in them for long periods or to abandon the real work we have already started (which requires genuine effort).

Reading a medium-sized book can take several days, while writing a novel, working on a project plan, or creating a painting may take several months before being presented to the public. And even then, there may be some praise, giving us a sense of accomplishment of real work. However, this is often not satisfying enough for us without continuous praise and recognition.

On the other hand, sharing a selfie or two, or a picture with a book, or a picture in a state of apparent inattention (commonly understood as posing to project a certain attitude while pretending to be authentic) on social media platforms quickly brings positive feedback with compliments from others and further interaction. In the same month that we need to work on an important project but remain invisible to the public, we can send thirty daily pictures to receive wonderful psychological rewards from others. Here is where the addiction to these feelings develops.

And the question is, can an ordinary person withstand this waste of real work time – with uncertain outcomes – in exchange for having a way to receive small and ongoing bursts of psychological satisfaction through social media channels or by sharing trivial matters with others?

How can we persuade, for example, a young and well-known individual on Twitter or one of the Snapchat influencers who constantly appear and interact with their followers throughout the day, that in order to accomplish real work (which may have a lasting impact even after completion), they must dedicate a significant portion of their day, relinquishing many immediate gratifications obtained from their followers, in order to engage in real work that may succeed, fail or hold value?

Why do we smile for social media pictures?

Because at that moment, we are in front of the camera, not facing reality.

I distinctly remember moments when I took pictures with a big smile alongside others. Those few seconds captured in the photo become immortalized on my social media accounts for months and even years. Such pictures repeat themselves, and someone else might see how many happy pictures I have and perhaps envy those brief moments of smiles in front of the camera, not realizing the reality.

When I look at a picture of someone on social media, amid a large group of "smiles", I know this person must have bigger problems beyond the number of likes. I often try to analyze the purpose behind posting these (unreal) photos, showcasing a rich life to the world. I wonder, is it an escape or a way to seek positive comments as an outlet?

Our smiling pictures don't reflect reality, that's true. However, they serve as an important source of dopamine, the easiest food for the ego. Sharing them is not the main problem, but let's try to smile more in real life than in front of the camera.

Instant Happiness and Human Evolution

In general, we want things now instead of later. There is a lack of psychological comfort with self-denial (when we don't get things immediately). From an evolutionary perspective, our instinct is to seize the readily available reward rather than the distant ones. In fact, resisting this impulse is difficult. Dr. Haythmet mentioned the concept of "instant gratification" in one of his publications and added, "Evolution (genetic and environmental) contributed to giving humans and other animals a strong desire to focus on getting immediate rewards. In human environments (early human life), food availability during the day was uncertain, similar to the rest of the animal world."

He adds, "Due to our natural instinct as humans (which has been passed down through generations) to survive and reproduce, we have a strong inclination to seize things and possessions that are smaller or weaker than us (like hunting and using tools available in the environment) as soon as they appear. This is precisely what represents instant rewards."

For us, immediate happiness or gratification is better than waiting for long periods for psychological satisfaction. It can be seen as analogous to the food that primitive humans sought, saying to themselves, "Why wait when I can have it now?

"I want to eat now, and anything I find, I will grab it immediately." This is what the contemporary person says. "I want to feel joy and appreciation for myself right now, and any behaviour that brings me this feeling, I will do it immediately."

From this statement, we understand that the main driving force for this behaviour is instinctive, more than just a result or product of technological advancements (even in the desire for instant happiness instead of tangible objects). However, technology has undoubtedly amplified and led this to levels that can be considered extreme. This instinct is the main driving force and the biggest reason for the success of online entertainment channels, as they mostly aim to satisfy the individual's needs for instant gratification.

We find that everyone's eagerness to follow social media channels and share numerous pictures stems from various internal motivators, including:

1. A quick source to stimulate a bored mental state (entertainment).
2. A fast source to try to treat distress (depression).
3. A rapid source to seek immediate praise (even if it's praise for fake achievements) or to enhance the ego rather than focusing on real problems.

Psychiatrist M. Scott Peck (1978) beautifully captures another perspective about our attempts to avoid real challenges in our lives. "This inclination to ignore problems is once again a simple manifestation of an unwillingness to delay gratification. Confronting problems is, as I have said, painful. To willingly confront a problem early, before we are forced to confront it by circumstances, means to put aside something pleasant or less painful for something more painful. It is choosing to suffer now in the hope of future gratification rather than choosing to continue present gratification in the hope that future suffering will not be necessary."

In other words, it is better for you to choose to endure hardship now, with the hope of satisfaction in the future, than to continue the current gratification in the hope future hardship won't be necessary. This analogy suggests we tend to seek immediate gratification in various aspects of our lives, instead of focusing on real challenges that require immediate action, causing us to delay them until later.

Peck further states, "Sometimes it seems to us that a salesman who ignores clear problems in his profession is emotionally or psychologically immature. But I say that this man we see is every man, and his apparent immaturity exists in all of us. One of the top generals in the army mentioned this to me, confirming this matter: 'The biggest problem in this army, as I believe it is in any organization, is that most officials continue to sit and look at the problems in their work, even staring directly at them, and they don't do anything about it, as if these problems will magically disappear if they sit still for long enough.' This general was not talking about a state of mental weakness or abnormality; he was talking about other generals and high-ranking officials – mature men in capacity and stability, trained in discipline."

The same applies to parents and out-dated executives. Although they are usually unprepared for it, their task can always be complex such as managing a company or dealing with other partners. Like executives in the army, most parents also tend to look at the problems in their relationships with their children for months or even years before taking any effective action, if they take any action at all.

What Peck mentions focuses on the automatic behaviour of humans, where they avoid addressing the underlying challenges and problems they face, opting instead for things that provide them with instant gratification. He believes that adopting true long-term discipline towards our lives and responsibilities is what enables us to approach our problems rationally and calmly, rather than relying on quick fixes.

Peck says, "Life is difficult. This is a great truth, one of the greatest truths. Once we truly see this truth, we transcend it. And once we have faced it, life is no longer difficult afterward. The whole thrust of my books has been to convince people that life is difficult, that this is a great truth, and that one of the consequences of this truth is that we must work very hard to grow, to be more fully human, to transcend our pain by cooperating with the truth."

He adds, "The tendency to avoid problems and the emotional suffering inherent in them is the primary basis of all human mental illness. Since most of us tend to avoid problems one way or another, most of us have some degree of mental illness. Some of us go to greater lengths than others to avoid problems and suffering, distancing ourselves from anything that is clear and reasonable to attempt to find easier solutions, sometimes completely detaching ourselves from reality."

When Peck talks about discipline, he means that when we teach ourselves and our children discipline, we are teaching them how to endure hardship and how to grow in their lives.

As for these tools or methods for dealing with suffering, or what I call "discipline", I summarize them in four kinds of behaviour: delaying gratification, accepting responsibility, dedication to truth and achieving balance.

Peck emphasizes that these are not complex tools that require extensive training. On the contrary, they are simple tools that almost all children master before the age of ten.

INSTANT HAPPINESS AND HUMAN EVOLUTION

He says, "Truth or reality is avoided when it is painful. We can revise our maps only when we have the discipline to overcome that pain. To have such discipline, we must be totally dedicated to truth. That is to say that we must always hold truth, as best we can determine it, to be more important, more vital to our self-interest, than our comfort. Conversely, we must always consider our personal discomfort relatively unimportant and, indeed, even welcome it in the service of the search for truth. Mental health is an ongoing process of dedication to reality at all costs."

Procrastination and the Instant Happiness Monkey

Continuing the issue of instant happiness in its contemporary form, blogger and renowned writer Tim Urban discussed his eternal struggle with procrastination in his blog and his TED Talk. He described his ongoing battle with procrastination since his university days when he was assigned a research project that required months of effort throughout the academic semester. However, procrastination led him to postpone this task until the end of the semester and rush to complete the challenging project within seventy-two hours, producing a poor result. I believe this story is familiar to many.

What happened to Urban was his preoccupation, as he described it, with a fictional character he named the "Instant Happiness Monkey." This character encouraged him to engage in activities that brought only immediate happiness (social media, browsing Wikipedia, hanging out with friends, and other distractions) without focusing on tasks that required greater effort and had long-term rewards, such as the research project. Then, one day, he met another character he called "Panic Monster" who informed him that it was time to submit the project or accomplish the goals that were supposed to be long-term and turn them into difficult and short-term tasks. The monkey would disappear, overwhelmed by the Panic Monster, and he would be left alone with this creature that compelled him to complete the task quickly, attempting to accomplish as much as possible in a short time, without quality or clear value in the project.

Urban's depiction of the monkey in relation to the concept of instant happiness was insightful. Traditional monkey behaviour, if we imagine it, never focuses on what we call long-term goals. Monkeys eat, drink, play, and constantly seek "instant happiness" without caring about what will happen tomorrow, as they have no future achievement ambitions.

If we think about it realistically, we will find that humans are among the few creatures blessed by God with the ability to think about long-term goals. Moreover, the primary instinct within humans forms in their early years and develops (or diminishes) in the pursuit of greater long-term gains compared to immediate gains if the options are available, just as we used to postpone delicious treats until the end when we were younger.[1]

Here, mention is made of the famous "Marshmallow Test," supervised by Dr. Walter Mischel since the 1970s, which focused significantly on the concept of "delayed gratification". In short, children were presented with two options: the first was to take a cookie or a marshmallow now, and the second was to wait for fifteen minutes and receive a larger quantity of them. Some children opted for the immediate reward, while others showed the ability to

---

[1] It may be worth exploring the radical difference in interaction between these two instincts: the immediate instinct that drives humans to continue living and the delayed gratification instinct that motivates them not to seek immediate joy secretly. The difference arises when all the options are actually available to humans. They tend to postpone the happier options, similar to what children do. Here, we come to distinguish between the concepts of "need" and "desire".

delay gratification and chose the second option. This study led to a classic and well-known result in the scientific world that may be challenging for us to apply as adults (though not impossible). The finding indicates that children who possess the ability to delay their happiness (by choosing the second option) tend to have better opportunities for success in the future compared to their peers.

Even though delayed gratification generally applies better to children than adults, it saddens me to say that one of the most critical factors influencing decisions in seeking immediate versus delayed happiness is social (from the influence of the surrounding environment), not just instinctive needs like the basic human need for food and drink.

Perhaps we can claim that since childhood, humans clearly express their material needs, such as crying to indicate the need for sleep or food. However, their young minds cannot manage these needs by obtaining them daily; they merely express the need. This highlights the difference between feelings and clear interaction. I believe the problem with adults lies in their interaction with their needs, not merely expressing them.

Public Status

"The first principle is that you must not fool yourself, and you are the easiest person to fool."
~Richard Feynman

What drives us to seek instant gratification?

1. Fear of Missing Out (FoMO)[2]: The individual's sense, following news and other social matters, that they are not imitating what is happening in public or other people's private lives leads them to worry or fear that they are missing something important that others possess (information). Instant gratification is achieved whenever the individual is eager to fulfill a hidden desire by keeping up with others, even in the pursuit of knowledge. If the individual does not acquire it, they may feel isolated or left behind.

2. The search for love or appreciation: When we mentioned

---

2 Fear of Missing Out:

FoMO is a condition that drives people to desire constant connection for fear of missing out on events in which they are not participating. For most individuals with social media accounts, this can cause anxiety or distress due to the fear of losing a social connection or missing out on important happenings. This condition emphasizes that the sense of connection or bonding with others is a legitimate psychological need that affects people's mental well-being.

See: Shea, Michael (27 July 2015). "Living with FoMO." The Skinny.

the case of an individual feeling distressed after sharing an expression with others, the main motivation behind that is self-satisfaction through obtaining the admiration of others for the situation (even if it does not necessarily address the root cause of the distress). In other cases, individuals seek appreciation with positive intentions, hoping for acceptance, love or care from others.

These two cases can be considered significant drivers for seeking social status. Perhaps one of the easiest ways to achieve this is by sharing with others what we do throughout our day, such as taking pictures of our meals, the books we read, new clothes we bought or even capturing smiles of ourselves, our children and our pets.

There is no real flaw here from my point of view. However, I believe the problem arises when we mix the triviality of these shares with other, more profound matters, such as sharing our achievements or what we consider accomplishments, which leads to the concept of the "illusion of achievement" I mentioned earlier.

When we attend an event or a party, or even if one of us does a simple TV interview on an unknown channel, we will post pictures of it on social media. We may not initially think about emphasizing the importance or reason behind the interview or the presence at that event, as much as we care about telling others that we did it, in order to gain approbation.

Here, I connect this interaction with the mentioned drivers; by informing everyone that we are just like them (going out, attending celebrations, trying new restaurants), and also giving them a reason to make us deserve appreciation and attention. Our language implicitly says, "Look, I did a TV interview and attended a self-development workshop…

it makes me feel worthy of some attention, please."

"The ego, or how people view themselves, can be likened to an inflated balloon that remains so forever, and the air inside the balloon acts as the helium of external love from others, keeping the balloon inflated. The smallest pin approaching the balloon will lead us to feel ignored." This is how Alain de Botton describes "the self" in his book "Status Anxiety".

* * * *

Like other people, I have, and still do, share on social media channels the events in which I participate. But the discussion point I now bring to the table is different, followed by the most important question that I want to explore in this book about the concept of work: Does what we share actually add value to others and genuine value to us? And the other question: Do we care about having value in the first place, or is the purpose of sharing merely to express our lives? If it is merely to express ourselves, I don't think there is a fault in the equation but I fear that our sharing of interactions related to our work and aspirations may continue to bring a sense of "illusion of achievement" to both us and others. They might see us as more important individuals and we might feel deserving of the attention we should have received (otherwise, we wouldn't have shared it with others in the first place).

The other crucial question is: Did our work or presence at that event, interview, workshop, or purchase of something actually provide equ1ivalent benefit or genuine value? And if it did, did we share that true value with others, or did we just settle for sharing pictures?

Taking pictures of any books we own on the shelf is much easier than reading them, and summarizing and preparing material that others can benefit from is more challenging than simply reading them. There is a difference between photographing the book and sharing with others what we have gained from reading it. The difference lies in "the self" or the attempt to tell others that we deserve attention because we own new books.

The Ego and the Idea

The more the focus is on the idea and the value, the farther it moves away from personification and the "ego" fades away. Images and pictures are connected to us. Ideas and values belong to everyone.

If we ask a photographer attending a workshop on parenting what the most important ideas and lessons he took from it are, a follower may be enticed to discuss ideas and lessons rather than the images themselves. The discussion might evolve with the second and third participants until it turns into a valuable discussion worth publishing. The value increases when the image-owner takes care to document the experience by writing a detailed article or professionally recording a video about the most significant lessons learned. The video may remain on YouTube for years, benefiting others, and the detailed article may become the seed of a future book that benefits every reader. On the other hand, the images of those contributions, with comments like "Keep it up" or "Nice work," will disappear in the workshop with their owner's intention, nonchalantly.

The picture represents the "illusion of achievement," while the subsequent work represents "real work".

It is not hidden from the discerning reader that real work, even after attending a workshop like that, remains the most challenging, impactful, and important for the person concerned and those familiar with his/her lifestyle.

Reading the logic of the Public

The French physician, historian and psychologist Gustave Le Bon delved into the behaviour of the public in a large body of his research. From his writings (dating back several decades), we may extract insights into the collective mind's functioning in this matter. He explains:

"The general public thinks in images. These images in their minds lead them to other images and are not logically related to their true image. Rarely can the general public distinguish between attempting to achieve a personal goal and the greater purpose by imagining those images. They strongly accept the images drawn in their minds, although they are always far removed from reality. The general public can only think in the images in their minds, and they only find delight in them."

Le Bon's awareness of this phenomenon (since 1896) encompasses the connection between public behaviour and the images that exist in their minds, which significantly differ from the actual reality of the individual (and others) in real life. The mental image leads to behaviour that may justify actions that enhance the "self" in front of others. It can be said here that the sense of accomplishment represents the final image in the minds of individuals within the public. Consequently, all subsequent interactions arise, neglecting the reality underlying them.

Le Bon further elaborates, which can be understood

as a continuation: "We see then the disappearance of the conscious personality and the domination of the unconscious personality. Our personality changes through the infection of emotions and thoughts, so that we become like others, transforming the proposed ideas from the mind into immediate actions; and here we see in these characteristics the main features of the individual, which make him/her a part of the general public. The individual is no longer him/her but has become a person who refrains from self-guidance and self-management by their own will."

In other words, individuals are directly influenced and altered by being exposed to the ideas of others and this manifests instantaneously as unconscious behaviour. They then lose their ability to manage and guide themselves, as they transform from being unique individuals into mainstream parts of the public, who copy what others do without questioning the value of these actions.

This analysis is logical to a great extent, as it is natural for an individual to react in most cases by attempting to enhance the "self" if others have reacted in the same way before, alluding to the "illusion of achievement". Excessive posting and appearances on social media, while neglecting actions that provide real value to others, becomes an actual satisfaction that is much easier than actual effort.

Another problem with this conviction is that it portrays these participants as having achieved something significant in front of younger generations while rendering continuous interaction as the only path to success. It is common now to find teenagers who eagerly take pictures with famous personalities without being aware of their accomplishments or having benefited from them. If one were to ask them,

"What did you gain from taking a picture with that person?" we should not be surprised if they simply replied, "Because they are famous."

The eagerness for social status shifts from creating real value for them to settling for fame, even if it's just fame.

Social status

Everything I have discussed so far leads us to a simpler and more sensitive topic: the pursuit for social status.

Human nature often drives individuals to seek themselves through the eyes of others, and this may distract us from creating our own values only to replace them with attempts to polish our image, just like the one who polishes his car every day and neglects to take it for regular maintenance. Why? Because others' perception is more important.

The importance of social status for individuals does not change through achieving material accomplishments as much as through their ability to adapt themselves to their life, which passes through crises and achievements. To remain the same person in all circumstances and situations is key. The pursuit for social status, like many other emotions, can evolve and it is a matter of how to create values rather than seek fame.

And perhaps the saying "money changes people" can indeed be felt in a practical sense when it is measured against many individuals. It is not because others who have acquired wealth are necessarily bad people but rather because human nature changes and evolves with changes in their material situation. The real challenge lies in controlling oneself, showing humility and managing internal emotions related to the pursuit of social status during times of crisis and beyond.

Social media platforms are considered the best and easiest

tool for individuals to prove their social status to others. By posting numerous pictures with well-known figures and frequently wearing traditional clothing that signifies affluence, the person might give the silent observer the impression that they are one of the country's wealthiest businessmen or an important personality at the very least. However, one forgets that what they see are merely images, and the reality might be that the person is actually living paycheck to paycheck or even unemployed. Eventually, reality will assert itself when a person lacks wealth or influence that they can leverage with others in their lives. Consequently, they might use social media and other means to create a perception of social status that they strive to achieve in their minds.

The owner of a luxury wallet, the doctor and the vegetable merchant

I recall an incident when I used to work at a bank. One day, a customer visited me to close his bank account due to failure to update his information.

He seemed overly concerned about his appearance. When I asked him for his identification card to start the update process, he pulled out his wallet, which was a luxury brand and filled with bank cards, both from our bank and others.

I adjusted myself in my seat, fearing that the account holder was a high-net-worth individuals. However, to my surprise, his balance was merely a few thousand riyals. As I proceeded with questions related to the update, provided by the central bank (where do you work, what is your salary, do you have any other sources of income, where do you live, etc.), it was evident that the man was greatly bothered by my inquiry and ceased to reply. I tried to convince him that these questions were not personal. I said I meet dozens of clients every day without differentiating or memorizing their names and positions to pass judgment. Regardless, the gentleman persisted in refusing to disclose the information. Consequently, I had to involve the branch manager, who also tried to persuade the customer to answer my questions or risk not completing the update process.

The man felt embarrassed and told me he held an office manager position for one of the department heads in a reputable company. Of course, there was nothing wrong with that but I sensed from his hesitant response that he did not want to disclose his position, which did not align with his elegant attire and numerous bank cards. I remember he initially mentioned that his job was "a manager" but he did not mention that he was an office manager.

Anyway, his salary did not exceed five thousand riyals and he barely mentioned this information, which was personally irrelevant to anyone at the bank and certainly not of any concern to me, as important as it was to disclose it for the bank's database. The man's thoughts were in one valley, while my requests for disclosure were in another.

Today, I understand this man's keenness to present an image that did not reflect his true self. His behaviour was nothing more than an imitation of many of us in society. Perhaps his position, which requires constant communication with managers, businessmen and important figures on behalf of his direct supervisor, had influenced his internal emotions. These emotions tell him that he is like them and perhaps more important than them.

His eagerness to play this role of importance continued even outside his workplace. He forgot that he was, in reality, just an employee. He also forgot that we, too, were mere employees who wanted to finish our workday to return home for lunch or hookah.

How I hope that this man did not display this kind of behaviour with his friends, who might mock him, further exacerbating his conflicted psyche and leading him to engage in such posturing with strangers as a compensation for the lack he feels (as he did in our encounter).

I remember another client who, whenever he mentioned

THE OWNER OF A LUXURY WALLET,

the name of an important figure, would jump in to inform me that he either knows him or had dinner with him at some time. In less than an hour he repeated the same talking points at least five times, He claimed to have declined several positions, mentioning them one by one. I interrupted him and asked about his education to register it in the bank's system. He said, "A doctorate" but that "unfortunately" he had to withdraw before he could finish his thesis.

The vegetable merchant's story, in contrast, was entirely different. A humble and modestly dressed fifty-year-old man handed me his Ithbat (proof of identity for non-Saudis) from a sealed plastic bag. I do not recall the type of transaction he came for, but I remember that he could neither read nor write, and he did not possess a signature. He relied solely on his fingerprint to complete his banking transactions. To my surprise, when I accessed his account, I found that he was a "private banking" client. Furthermore, I was initially surprised that he did not go to the private banking department, only to discover that he did not even know the difference and did not care about it in any case.[3]

This gentleman had assets worth a few million riyals. When I asked him about his occupation, he told me that he was a vegetable and fruit merchant in the vegetable market and owned several refrigerators that he rented out. I served him and he bid me a warm farewell, leaving me astonished, especially since his visit coincided with those of the office

---

3 The "Ithbat" (identification) for resident brothers in the Kingdom at that time was a booklet resembling a passport and not like the national identity card or residency permit used today. Moreover, the booklet could be used multiple times if it was not torn or damaged, as was the case with the protagonist of the story.

manager and the doctor.

Dozens of similar cases have left me bewildered by their contradictions and differences. Those I cite here may appear peculiar but they represent members of society. I may unwittingly be one of them, or they may be a cousin, brother or close relative to someone I know.

Like working at a bank or being a doctor, these occupations require delving into the hidden depths of the human psyche. In this book, I am trying to shed light on some of the hidden beliefs and behaviour, aiming to focus on the larger goal: to emphasize real matters and actions that demand more attention. Through this, we hope to contribute to the transformation of someone, somewhere, for the better.

"To be yourself in a world that is constantly trying to make you something else is the greatest accomplishment."

Ralph Waldo Emerson
American essayist, lecturer and philosopher, 1803–1882

About Appearances and Initial Impressions

Scene One: In early 2016, two of my friends organized two grand celebrations to mark the opening of their respective stores or businesses. A significant portion of the attendees consisted of media personnel and social media influencers. Numerous photos were posted on their accounts showcasing the details of these openings, with more pictures featuring my friends alongside their friends (and their friends' friends), all adorned with smiles and accompanied by well-wishers in the comments section. The ultimate goal was to give the viewers a strong sense of success for these new brands even before they had officially begun.

Scene Two: In 2009, a television program team from a well-known channel visited my home for the purpose of conducting a full-length interview with me (lasting about forty-five minutes) after being recommended by a dear brother to whom I am grateful. During the interview, I answered many questions about my private start-up business.

Of course, what concerned me, first personally and secondly concerning my work, were my answers to the many questions asked by the presenter. The TV crew included cameramen, an assistant director, a lighting technician, and the elegant and gracious presenter.

My parents were in awe (I wasn't married at the time, so the interview took place at my parents' house). Amid all the commotion of setting up for the interview, the host even asked my mother if she was my sister. It was a surprise to her, considering my relatively young age.

I remember clearly the living room of our house was turned upside down to accommodate the filming of that program. As I write these words today, several years after that interview, I have to admit that the company I had founded closed its doors in 2012 due to my lack of experience in managing it. I was in my early twenties and I didn't have the cash flow to sustain the business. Another factor was that the partners did not have full confidence in the company. In reality, it was far from being a success story, as it had seemed at the time of the interview.

Regarding Scene One, I regret to say one of the companies closed down in less than a year due to the absence of even half an indication of success. The owners of the second company are currently negotiating its sale to someone who possesses sufficient managerial and financial capabilities. All of this happened swiftly, while the photos from the openings remain fresh and present, even as I write these lines.

Photos are easy. Real accomplishments are difficult.

A REFLECTION ON STATUS AND MATERIALISM

Why you should distance yourself from school friends

"Alain de Botton" talks on multiple occasions about the concern of seeking social status.

For some people, this status increases according to the quantity of material possessions, such as luxury cars, expensive watches or designer clothes. Status could also stem from holding important professional positions, like ambassadors, executives or businessmen. The way people see themselves and their level of self-confidence often correlates with their possessions.

The ironic point that de Botton mentions is that none of us felt jealous of Queen Elizabeth I despite her wealth and position, both surpassing ours by a wide margin. This is because we had no direct personal connection with her. We saw her on television and heard about her, but we never met her in person. She was not part of the close social circle that drives us to compare ourselves or feel jealous. This contrasts with how we feel towards our peers and people who are part of our social circles.

The majority of people are keen on boosting their self-confidence and this drives us to compare ourselves constantly to others, especially friends. The strong desire to feel that we need more admiration and appreciation sometimes leads us to make sacrifices in order to obtain something from it, like spending money we desperately need to buy expensive shoes to show off.

When people truly believe they are unique and complete in themselves, their attachment to material possessions and positions diminishes because they are content with who they are and their current state. However, it's easier said than done.

De Botton believes the main reason that drives us to seek self-worth through material possessions or things that are not necessarily important is due to the presence of arrogant personalities in our lives. Through these individuals, we see our own shortcomings and are influenced by them, pushing us to chase after less important matters and neglect our true essence.

By contrast, relationships with our mothers are different. They don't care about our appearance or status. A mother's perspective towards children is purely humane. Her encouragement for them and standing by their side to attain material possessions is, in essence, the same motivation as that of the arrogant individuals.

De Botton makes a serious point in a humorous way, when he points out that one of the worst encounters that happens in our society is meeting classmates years after graduation.

This is simply because it compels us to compare ourselves with the same person who was mostly similar to us in life circumstances and age. This can strongly undermine our self-confidence when we realize that the lazy classmate now possesses more wealth and holds a higher position.

Here I would like to comment on the topic of encounters

and interactions. The ability for each one of us to fill our self-confidence tank and be content with what we have, disregarding what we lack, is a good step before planning for any meeting. Whether it's a school reunion or any other social gathering.

Through this discussion, I fear readers might get the impression that I am completely against seeking social status or buying expensive clothes and cars. That's not true. I must admit with some shyness that, from my point of view, German cars and some expensive clothes often come with higher quality compared to cheaper alternatives. In fact sometimes, if my financial situation allows, I do purchase them. However, my argument here is not to divert attention from the desired social status that everyone may aspire to, nor is it against material possessions and titles, as much as it is an attempt to search for self-worth through matters that are more important, realistic and valuable to ourselves and others, and not to pursue social status solely for the sake of others.

In essence, I am trying to emphasize the idea of focusing more on our work than on appearances. I remind myself and others that work endures and creates value, while appearances and showcasing ourselves as something we are not lead to negative and even deceitful levels of self-perception.

None of us should try to approach such an idea even if it involves exposing minor flaws, instead of covering up major ones, using pretence.

Secondly, it claims to achieve what I have been trying to explain subconsciously from the beginning, which is the "illusion of achievement" and reinforcing the "self". Otherwise, most of us wouldn't be preoccupied with it and neglect more important matters.

Hatoon Kadi and Social Status[4]

I1 discussed on my Snapchat the issue of fame, being in the spotlight and how painful it is for people to compare themselves to others based on fame, spotlight and wealth. I said this kind of thinking can be disastrous because there are many exceptional and talented individuals in every field. Especially in professions and specialized fields where it is important for a person to stand out within their circle. For example, the measure of academic excellence may be the ability to publish research in high-ranking journals, and a doctor's distinction may come from good reputation among colleagues and patients, as well as commitment to personal development. This applies to every field.

The response to my post made me think deeply. I was initially shocked by the reality of how a doctor, who holds such a noble profession and is known for having a high income, can compare herself to any famous person in any field. I don't underestimate the value of anyone but the comparison is unfair (and not objective) because there is no common ground between them. I wonder why the person

---

4 I had the honour of being joined by the well-known media personality Hatoon Kadi (host of the program "Noon Al-Nisan"), who generously devoted her time to have a rich discussion with me about the concept of seeking social status, especially among young women in our society. She participated with me in this section of the book, and for that, I extend my heartfelt thanks.

who wrote the message doesn't strive to develop herself further to excel as a surgeon.

I remember reading once that being a surgeon is one of the highest-paying professions in the world but it demands hard work and a lot of effort, what the woman doctor referred to as "akragha" (a local saying for hard work). In reality, this hard work is an essential aspect of a profession I once very much wanted to join. I hesitated when I realized the magnitude of responsibility and chose a different path for myself. Everyone who enters the medical profession knows in advance the level of effort required but they also know the happiness and satisfaction that comes from contributing to saving and improving people's lives, in addition to the social status. So why this constant talk of "exhaustion and fatigue"?

Exhaustion and fatigue are part of any profession. Or have we become people who desire money and wealth without effort? The success of an artist or any celebrity might be evident to everyone, as news of a successful event or marketing campaign fills social media because it is entertaining and easy-to-consume content. However, the impact of a doctor's work might be transplanting a life-saving organ to a person or making a successful diagnosis for someone a long time in pain. All of this is found in an outstanding and great profession. Then someone comes and compares it to celebrities?

Value yourselves, appreciate your efforts and don't compare them to anyone else's. If money and fame are the only measures of success, then why don't we all become dancers? I say this with all due respect for all.

Value yourselves because everything is made easy for what it was created for.

The response of a distinguished woman who is a successful

doctor was controversial regarding the previous post I wrote. She focused on comparing herself and her social status to a famous person on Snapchat who works as a makeup artist. There is no real flaw, to be honest, in the makeup artist's profession. Hatoon told me, "I encourage everyone in this world to pursue their passion and develop in it, and there's no need for comparisons with others in different fields." Here, it should be made clear that the difference in specialization does not imply that it falls within the bounds of comparison because both people are women, as Hatoon explained. The doctor's admiration for the makeup artist might be driven by the lights and fame the latter achieved, without considering the circumstances surrounding the makeup artist behind the Snapchat camera. Celebrities naturally only show what they want to show, and as the saying goes, "what's hidden might be even greater".

Social media professionals know that great challenges arise from the lack of a clear and direct method through which they can consistently earn a regular or even high income. The second challenge becomes apparent in the extent of compromises they have to make in many cases in order to promote products or companies they may not believe in. Necessity and continuity require compromises.

It is common knowledge that being famous or a celebrity entails a flood of constant praise and flattery, as well as insults and a lack of etiquette. This is another significant sacrifice that celebrities must make to continue their careers. Naturally, this is not an easy task for anyone, even if they are described as having "thick skin" by psychologists or being able to withstand psychological blows with high tolerance, being in that respect similar to how a body endures physical blows.

In another instance, Hatoon also shared a post (which may seem mocking, though I found it simultaneously profound and lighthearted) on her Instagram account about a societal issue (especially among Gulf nationals) regarding the "anxiety of seeking status". She stood to take a souvenir photo of herself in front of the famous Harrods store in London and wrote under the picture of her post: "In front of Harrods".

In front of Harrods department store

In front of this prestigious store in London lies the epitome of show-off and ostentation in the world. In front of "Harrods" and in the many streets surrounding it, you can see luxury cars. I don't know their names, so I remain ignorant in the eyes of those accompanying me. It's no wonder most of these cars bear Gulf license plates. You see "Don Juan" stepping out of his car, adorned from head to toe with brands, strutting as if he owns the world and everything in it. He heads towards Harrods to take his daily tour and concludes by sitting at one of the expensive cafes in Knightsbridge, where you see many, many Gulf nationals. But what goes on inside Harrods is a different story. This "Don Juan" with the luxury car will not accept his visit to various Harrods departments to be ordinary shopping. He casts glances here and there, seeking admiration from other Harrods shoppers, drowning in brands from the bag, clothes, to the Chanel brooch and Cartier and Cleef & Arpels jewelry.

The show-off culture in London is as ancient as London itself. There are always new wealthy individuals who do not feel satisfied with themselves unless they announce to the world that they are rich. They may not be empty; some of them are successful businessmen and businesswomen. However, the envious and admiring gazes from people give them a great sense of happiness, contentment and satisfaction. Initially, I used to feel embarrassed by their desperate desire to show off and I felt that it was my duty to explain to the world that we are not all like that, and that these individuals are a minority. But I discovered that my feelings are futile. Only fools believe that all Gulf nationals flaunt themselves at Harrods, just as fools believe that all Muslims are terrorists. So, why bother explaining?

I still see the theatrical displays in Harrods and the extravagant streets of London as ridiculous and poorly directed. However, I have lost all desire to demonstrate that we are not all like that. Let them show off and boast and one day they will realize that those whose most valuable possessions define them will die dissatisfied, as they are never content. When the human soul is released into its greed, it becomes like hell, for ever asking, "Is there more?"

And London remains the most beautiful city in human existence (in my opinion).

Alain de Botton has an additional opinion regarding the pursuit of social status through displaying wealth and proving the "self". It is based on a quote from the philosopher and author of "The Social Contract" Jean-Jacques Rousseau. He said, "Rousseau's argument hangs on a radical thesis. He says, 'To be rich, this does not require owning many things. Instead, it requires the individual to possess what he desires in his life'."

Wealth is not absolute. It increases or decreases based on human desire. Every time we desire something we cannot possess, we become poorer, regardless of the resources available to us. And every time we feel content with what we have, we become richer, even if what we possess is relatively little. There are two ways to make a person wealthier, according to Rousseau: give them more money or reduce their desires.

De Botton adds, "For the individual among us, attempting to earn more money may not be the most effective way to feel wealthy. Instead, we might do better to distance ourselves practically and emotionally from these attempts and from those we consider equals, who happen to be wealthier than us. Instead of trying to be bigger fish (wealthier than them), we can focus our energies on finding smaller ponds, where we can appear bigger."

He also encourages adopting the concept of the philosopher and physicist William James in seeking social status in another way, saying, "We may be content enough with little if that little is what we expect, and we may become miserable with much when we learn the desire for more."

"When we learn the desire to have everything, instead of annoying buyers, we might blame the society that persuaded them that buying decorated tanks is necessary and rewarding from a psychological perspective, while the respect of others was limited to displaying wigs (mocking the nobility of past centuries)... The history of luxury can be read more accurately as a record of emotional shock. It is the legacy of those who feel pressured by the contempt of others, adding objects to their naked selves in order to signal that they too are deserving of love," Alain de Botton comments.

The problem of seeking social status is not necessarily confined to social media channels; it may affect our interactions with others, according to Hatoon in her post. What I find most worthy of comment on this matter is the preoccupation of successful individuals with the illusion of achievement or attaining "social status" apart from their success in their field or in matters they already aspire to succeed in. It may be strange from a behavioural perspective for successful young

Gulf nationals to be preoccupied with proving personal success (or social status) by ensuring they consistently appear in front of the Harrods store in London or the café "Le Fouquet's" on the Champs-Élysées in Paris, adorned with brands, as if their efforts, achievements and accomplishments in real life do not warrant attention and satisfaction. Instead they become preoccupied with showing only what they want to reflect from the eyes of others, for their eyes.

We are driven to ensure that our names are recognized, our presence acknowledged and our viewpoints heard, while expecting others to treat our failures with leniency and our needs with consideration, as these factors contribute to our flourishing. In his analysis of the state of anxiety in the search for social status, de Botton points out, "The interest of others is important to us because we feel uncertain about our worth and, as a result, we tend to let their judgments play a decisive role in how we see ourselves... Our sense of identity is dependent on the judgments of those among whom we live. If our jokes are found funny, our confidence will soar. If we are praised by someone, we will feel highly esteemed. And if others avoid us, or appear indifferent to our joining them in a gathering, or seem uninterested in the nature of our work or position, this might lead us to feel deeply insecure or unimportant."

Moreover, de Botton adds, "We envy only those whom we feel we ought to be like, primarily members of the same group as ourselves for comparison. In fact, there are few successes that can't be equalled by what we ostensibly compare ourselves with."

Similarly, David Hume reflects on human nature (Edinburgh, 1739) and its inclination towards envy, stating,

IN FRONT OF HARRODS DEPARTMENT STORE

"There is not a great difference between us and others who produce envy but quite the opposite; we feel closer to them. A soldier does not envy his peers as much as he would envy his commander." He emphasizes that significant disparities in positions can sever relationships and hinder us from approaching what we can attain, thereby weakening the positive effect of comparison.

The search for social status and the attempt to prove it is inherited from our ancestors

Until the mid-eighteenth century, the nobility and socially privileged class were clearly distinguished in Western societies, favouring the nobles and the wealthy over others. This distinction extended to all aspects, including non-financial ones such as politics, sciences and literature, creating a noticeable divide. The aim was to rely more on the most talented among the youth and rising generations for the future of civilization, rather than solely depending on their social backgrounds.

The beginning of this shake-up came at the hands of Thomas Paine, a human rights advocate and one of the founding fathers of the United States. In his book "Rights of Man" (1791), Paine made his mark with the following observation:

"I smile to myself when I contemplate that irony, the irony that will engulf literature and all sciences, as they attempt to make it hereditary... an inconsistent legacy, like the inheritance of writing. I don't know whether Homer or Euclid had children, but I will venture to express my opinion that if they left their works unfinished, then their offspring couldn't complete them."⁵

If science or literature is the projection that Thomas Paine made, the present audience can easily apply this principle to all other sectors, such as business management or family matters in our Arab society.

Napoleon Bonaparte consequently followed Thomas Paine's method and he took it to a new level that can be said to have changed the social and class map in the world, not just those of France and, more broadly, of Europe.

In the early days of his rule, he became the first Western leader to move explicitly towards a new system known as "available positions for talent". Napoleon described it as "I made most of my generals protected by it" and he proudly said in St. Helena towards the end of his life, "Whenever I found talent, I rewarded it."

With Napoleon, France witnessed the abolition of feudal privileges and honorific institutions, which were reserved for enhancing the status of the nobles and wealthy individuals, as well as the reformation of its education system, making

---

5   1.to note

One might argue that my focus on documentation and research is more centred on experiences in Western societies than on those we face in our local communities. There are two reasons for this. Firstly, projecting the lives of nobles and the wealthy in Western society is safer for the writer than delving into contemporary local cases, which could lead some readers to make negative associations or interpret it as a personal attack on a specific family or tribe. Thus, I wish to distance the audience from any personalization of the book's topics.

Secondly, I find it easier and more practical to document experiences from Western society and mention their sources. Moreover, I believe that the accumulation of Western experiences have a greater impact on the current lives of Arabs from my perspective. The idea remains essential and there are significant similarities in societies despite their differences in characteristics.

the Lycée[6] accessible to all.

In 1794, "École des Arts et Métiers" (School of Applied Arts) was established in France, and generous state grants were given to provide financial support for poor students. In its early years, half of the enrolled students were sons of peasants and craftsmen. Many prominent figures during Napoleon's rule came from humble backgrounds, among them his ministers and scientific advisors, and members of the Senate. In his famous description of the nobles, Napoleon justified this step by saying, "They are a curse to the nation and they are fools by inheritance."

Even after his downfall, Napoleon's ideas persisted and continued to influence Europe and the United States. Ralph Waldo Emerson expressed his desire to convey this notion in his vision that "every man should be placed in his right place. He must carry with him strength and self-confidence to use in his life."

Thomas Carlyle, the Scottish historian, philosopher and mathematician, for his part, was angry at the way the children of the wealthy squandered their wealth while the poor were deprived of even basic education. He wrote, "What shall we say about the idle aristocrats? The landowners in England, whose well-acknowledged profession was that they take good advantage of rent money. They consume well and shoot bullets into the air (in a satirical reference to their depletion of resources)," and he added, "I am against those who did not do anything useful, or from whom no one

---

6   Lycée is an innovative French educational system that covers students aged between 15 and 18. It was later named "La Deuxième Étape" (The Second Stage), where this phase aims to prepare students, if they wish, for the stage that follows, the Baccalaureate, which gives them the opportunity to learn in advanced levels or prepare them for professional life.

else benefited. Those who did not make any serious efforts to prove themselves in any field but instead inherited their privileges, entitlements and titles on a silver platter."

He drew a typical picture of the English aristocrat as one who "rises in his splendour; is exempt from work, need and danger. He sits calmly amid his devices and tools and other men perform all his tasks. And such a man calls himself noble." His father and ancestors worked for his benefit in the past, or as he himself said, "perhaps they gambled successfully just for him. And for him, this is the law of life and he actually believes that the law of the universe does not require him to do any tasks or that he must perform or accomplish, except for achieving pre-cooked victories, while being careful not to throw himself out of the window."

Alain de Botton comments on this again: "Like many reformers in the 19th century, Carlyle did not dream of a world in which everyone is equal financially but rather one that grants everyone (their social status) in their ascent and descent based on inequality. Europe requires a true aristocracy."

And, as Carlyle wrote, "Aristocracy should be limited to talents only. False aristocracy should never be supported." What he imagined was a system not yet named: merit.

Historically, the beginning of this call for class revival was initiated by one of the founding fathers of the United States, which later became evident in contemporary American culture. Unlike other civilizations in Europe and the Ottoman Empire which were characterized by significant class divisions, individuals from other societies were eager to associate themselves with the upper class, gradually leading them to do what they needed to become one of them. On the other hand, I must honestly say that American society, in general, does not tend towards such classism. You find lawyers, engineers, doctors and exceptionally wealthy businessmen generally not inclined to boast merely about their position, profession or financial status, and we haven't heard of a phenomenon of lineage and pedigree among them. Even though I have reservations about the recent racial history, which barely ended in the early 1970s, the American system deserves fair recognition. If needed, even if it requires a display or bragging, they will make their achievements a source of pride.

In the United States, the principle of equal opportunity for the public was established with an intended commitment to its implementation. In March 1961, less than two months after taking office, President John F. Kennedy Jr. established a committee on equal employment opportunity and tasked it with ending discrimination of all forms in government agencies and private companies. It was followed by a set of supporting laws, such as the Equal Pay Act of 1963, the Civil Rights Act of 1964, the Equal Employment Opportunity Act of 1964, the Older Americans Act of 1965, the Age Discrimination in Employment Act of 1967, the Equal Credit Opportunity Act of 1976, and the Americans with Disabilities Act of 1990. With such legislation, it was reasonable to believe that regardless of a person's age, religion, colour or gender, they would be guaranteed a fair and equal chance at success.

Adding to his commentary, de Botton reflects on these radical social changes, stating, "When the wealthy were still dominating the forefront of previous generations due to their family backgrounds or social connections, it was natural to reject the idea that wealth was an indicator of virtue, merely because some were born rich. However, even in a world of merit and just deserts, where prestigious positions and salaries could only be secured through real-life tests and individual capabilities, money has become a tool to display human greatness. The wealthy are not just wealthier; they seem to consider themselves inherently better than others."

In another context, he continues, "Many thanks to the valuable principle of merit. It has given the common people a chance to prove themselves. Talented and intelligent individuals from the common ranks, who have been confined to an immobile hierarchical framework for centuries, are now free to express their talents on a theoretical level. Background, gender, race, or age are no longer obstacles before this progress, and indeed, the element of justice has finally entered into the distribution of rewards."

However, there is also a dark aspect to this story, unfortunately, for those who occupy a lower social status. Another principle has emerged: if the successful succeed, it may necessarily follow that the failures they experience deserve their misfortune. In the era of merit and just deserts, it appears that an element of justice has not entered into the distribution of wealth between the poor and the wealthy. Low social status (as perceived) is not only unfortunate but also deemed as deserving.

There is no doubt that achieving financial success in the era of economic meritocracy, without benefiting from inheritance or privileges from birth, has become an unprecedented measure to validate the nobility of a person. Those who were given their wealth and castles by their fathers have been replaced by a new breed of individuals who attained success through their own merit. At the same time, financial failure has become associated with a sense of shame, mirroring the plight of the socially disadvantaged in ancient times who were deprived (practically and realistically) of all opportunities in life. These individuals, despite their unfortunate circumstances, were lucky enough to have escaped this dilemma.

The question arises: why does it happen? If someone is talented, intelligent and capable of achieving great things but remains poor, the impact of this condition is harsher and more painful for them, especially in the context of the new era of meritocracy.

From a personal analysis, the answer to this question seems to lie in how society views the poor, often with two demeaning perspectives. Firstly, they are seen as "naturally failing" and, secondly, they are considered "worthy of sympathy and recipients of charitable donations".

With the current technological and civilizational advancements, these perspectives have not necessarily become clear or evident to everyone. It is not easy for anyone to simply notice the struggles of their friends facing financial challenges. Their appearance may seem ordinary, they might own a car (even if not a luxury model), and they eat and drink normally.

It is worth noting here that most individuals from the lower or middle-income segments of society earnestly attempt to escape the appearance of relative poverty altogether. At the same time, they strive to prove their worthiness for respect and love in the era of meritocracy, as coined by de Botton, because poverty signifies failure to them. They do not want to be seen as failures, so they employ all available means to demonstrate not only that they are not failures but that they are successful in their lives, even if it requires certain compromises and sacrifices. Just as we present our best selves on social media, which may not reflect our true reality, many of us also indulge in buying luxury or unnecessary items to prove the opposite of our actual situation, even if it comes at the cost of significant financial sacrifices.

For the individual, the struggle is not merely a tussle between poverty and wealth, but rather a struggle to claim entitlement and tell others that we are fine, successful and wonderful, or that we are just like them or even better. We deserve appreciation, respect and admiration, even if it is superficial.

In summary, the driving force that compels the public to strive for social status can be attributed to two main factors:

1. Fear of being categorized within the realm of poverty: Poverty implies failure and lacking material needs, along with a deficit in social connections (even if proven through social media channels), indicating that they are considered "insignificant" in this life.
2. Meritocracy: While not everyone dreams of being a king, the search for people's recognition indirectly, showing that they are important, worthy and deserving of respect, leads them to resort to shortcuts like acquiring luxury brands, buying houses above their means, associating with influential figures on social media and, of course... documenting their presence at workshops and meetings that hold some significance, taking plenty of photos and sharing them.

What is controversial to me is that the pursuit of social status through shortcuts instills various beliefs within individuals in our societies. Often, they are not fully conscious of whether their actions hold true value or not, nor do they accurately gauge the importance of their actual accomplishments. Resentment can extend to the point where we find ourselves caught between the love of ostentation and fear of the evil eye, as humorously stated by someone.

Rarely does anyone pause to look at themselves in the mirror and ask, "Am I genuinely satisfied with myself?" Or do they try to find true worth through hard work, perseverance and self-esteem, seeking genuine merit and deserving recognition. Instead, most of us tend to opt for shortcuts, less effective in securing true worth.

"My God, if they knew the truth," were the words of the renowned novelist Gabriel Garcia Marquez when he was told he was being awarded the Nobel Prize for Literature. He was living in the opposite state of seeking social status. He believed that what he had done throughout his life didn't live up to the level of that status, extending beyond the facade. He considered his works "illusory achievements." Now, the world knows, after his death, that he actually lived a genuine life in which he left a profound impact in his own way.

Talking about social status is easy

"Since most men are not very good nor very wise, it is necessary to rely more on severity than compassion," says Italian historian Francesco Guicciardini (1486-1549).

Guicciardini's assumed severity applies to oneself and to those close to them in their pursuit of social status, regardless of its form. It is not the contemporary severity of physical beating or mockery in its literal sense but rather a severity towards oneself and those close to them concerning that status.

One form of this severity is the poor financial management of a person with themselves. It takes another form in the difficulty of allowing a young man to marry women from a lower social background or not attempting to approach certain communities without first proving their worthiness.

It is not difficult for the reader to realize that many cases of "different lineage and social status" have had a harsh impact on some simple couples, leading to their separation, as happened (and happens) in our local courts. One might boast about the unimportance and futility of such tribal or caste-based cruelty, also referred to as "social class differences", but for a father, for example, it is easier to overlook the personal merit of his daughter's suitor compared to his social class, color or position. And "merit" is still not the decisive factor in such matters. It is easier to talk than to act, especially when we try to measure it against our reality.

The most important matter is the existing social status

The most problematic and challenging issue with class privileges is that humans who possess them rarely give them up without being compelled to do so.

It is rare to find someone from the noble classes or individuals with prestigious titles in various societies who do not seek to use the privileges they were born with.

Imagine that since childhood, certain individuals give you an aura of respect, status and admiration that continues into adulthood. What will happen then is that the equation of "merit" and the pursuit of status through learning and hard work may not be as enticing as the allure it creates for those in the lower classes who do not possess social privileges and were not born with them. Even if you manage to achieve merit through hard work, it may be met with a sense of resignation from most of your peers.

Sometimes, social status acquired effortlessly remains the last lifeline for individuals to prove themselves if they lose everything. The more important equation then becomes the desire to claim social entitlement, which becomes more important than striving for success or persevering for merit.

If I fail in my professional life to attain recognition, I would resort to using the bestowed title or utilize my connections or the social privilege into which I was born.

In theory, we believe we don't care much for achieving social status but it is hard to deny it within ourselves before deciding whether we criticize it or not in others.

The pursuit of social status (through borrowing)

In an article entitled "Your Purchases Don't Bring You Social Status," the website "Done by Forty" mentions the search for status by trying to convince others that we are better than our actual circumstances by buying things we cannot afford. And the mention goes:

"With the ability to make purchases through borrowing, many of us have become engaged in a great deception. This occurs when we spend more than we actually earn, to the point where we have to borrow to compensate afterwards. Based on what we do professionally or what job we have, we may give the impression that we have more income than we actually receive. As a society, we buy more than our actual capabilities. Ironically, all of this is an attempt to convince ourselves and each other that we can easily afford all these things we have purchased."

The average person may not realize the effects of borrowing because it is one of the most important secrets for a family or a working individual, and this aspect becomes even more hidden when a person becomes accustomed to borrowing from a credit card month after month to convince others and themselves that they are in good shape and to prove that they have the ability to be like or better than some others they aspire to become.

The editors of the website add, "Why do we do this to

ourselves? We do it because we have been programmed to search for status (in an illusory way)". Add to that what David McCraney shares: "And because we are not very smart."

There is a part of the brain that believes it is very important to maintain our social position and our sense of belonging to a certain economic class more than preserving our limited income. And so, we go about trying to deceive each other with everything, from the clothes and jewellery we buy to our cars and homes. Each one of us competes to be the most middle-class family in the neighbourhood.

But why should I care?

Why does it matter if my neighbour (or friend) gains a little extra status by owning a second car in the driveway? I assume that the part that makes me wrong is precisely the idea that we can define the middle class through a set of purchases. This unfortunately seems realistic. However, we feel that the pursuit for social status – the one up for sale – (though many things) is specifically the fundamental reason for much of our poor financial behaviour.

It may not actually be the fault of advertisers or car manufacturers or clothing companies that we consume more than we need and far more than we can afford. Instead, we may bear a great responsibility because we believe that by purchasing these things, we secure a spot for our families in a respected social circle, or in a club where all the suitable members gather, and where we say to ourselves, it seems to us that everyone owns many things, and they have succeeded in achieving them for themselves. As if they are telling us, "Hey, we would be delighted if you joined us."

The editor of the website "Lifehacker," author Eric Ravenscraft, comments on this: "Of course, you can spend your money on whatever makes you happy. However, if the goal of spending is to seek status, you might get better returns by acquiring a new skill, improving your professional life or investing in your family. Spending to seek status through purchases will give you short-term fleeting results at best, but the status that comes from hard work or investing in time or with those around you is the most challenging."

The website "Done by Forty" aims to present the idea that deluding oneself into believing that status can be attained through lavish purchases and homes that cause us financial strain is based on two things, as I see them: "The illusion of accomplishment" and to prove "that we are not actually that smart." With editor Ravenscraft's comment, "Perhaps investing in the more meaningful things is the one that represents the real work, away from the crowd"; and with another supporting quote from de Botton on this matter, "Don't remind ourselves that shortly after reaching the summit (the peak of purchasing things and attaining status), we will descend again to the lowlands of anxiety and desire", we tend to believe that some achievements and possessions will give us lasting contentment."

Seeking social status without investing oneself in a specialization

When we see a person desperately seeking their status and appreciation from others through specialties and matters far from their professional or human achievements, it is worth noting that the sole motivation behind this individual is simply their lack of contentment with the life they are living. Their mind (or those around them in some cases) imagines that living the lives of others would make them a better person.

And it may be said without any flaw that the kind-hearted doctor (mentioned in the story of Hatoon) would not have chosen the medical profession if she had the options available to her without any financial or social pressures in her early days. Perhaps she dreamed of being a "makeup artist" or an "actress" or a "TV presenter." Here, I encourage the idea, before attempting to seek social status through easier and shorter means, that individuals should search for achievements that allow them to realize themselves and their place (and happiness), as well as add genuine value to others and those around them. It is not hidden from us that most successful people in the world are merely ordinary individuals in their reality and lives. Their sought-after positions are mostly realized through the lives they live in the real world, not through the illusions their imagination portrays to them.

"We notice clear evidence of both intelligence and foolishness, humor, confusion, importance and superficiality. In the midst of this mystery, we usually venture into the wider world to try to resolve the issue of our importance. Neglecting others highlights our self-evaluation and reveals the hidden negativity within us, whereas a smile or a compliment (from others) shows the opposite. It seems that we take into consideration that the impact of others makes us understand ourselves," comments Alain de Botton.

And as the great philosopher Arthur Schopenhauer, known for his pessimism, said:

"Our greatest happiness lies in being respected but those who respect us do not necessarily incline to express their respect, even if there are all possible reasons for it. Thus, the happiest person is the one who can sincerely respect himself, no matter what happens."

The problem with some positive people ... They target emotions only

"Our culture today is obsessively focused on unrealistically positive expectations: Be happier. Be healthier. Be the best, better than the rest. Be smarter, faster, richer, sexier, more popular, more productive, more envied and more admired," says Mark Manson, and he adds elsewhere:

"But when you stop and really think about it, conventional life advice— all the positive and happy self-help stuff we hear all the time — is actually fixating on what you lack. It lasers in on what you perceive your personal shortcomings and failures already are, and then emphasizes them for you. You learn about the best ways to make money because you feel you don't have enough money already. You stand in front of the mirror and repeat affirmations saying that you're beautiful because you feel as though you're not beautiful already. You follow dating and relationship advice because you feel that you're unlovable already. You try goofy visualization exercises about being more successful because you feel as though you aren't successful enough already. Ironically, this fixation on the positive—on what's better, what's superior—only serves to remind us over and over again of what we are not, of what we lack, of what we should have been but failed to be. After all, no truly happy person feels the need to stand in front of a mirror and recite that she's happy. She just is."

Manson adds, "There's a saying in Texas: "The smallest dog barks the loudest." A confident man doesn't feel a need to prove that he's confident. A rich woman doesn't feel a need to convince anybody that she's rich."

Mark Manson points out that the widespread nature of this culture (convincing others of your inadequacy) is very beneficial for commerce, as it constantly calls on you to hide your flaws by buying more things and compensating for the many fake deficiencies in you.

"The problem with excessive positive thinkers (some self-help gurus) is that they can be harmful to your mental health," concludes Manson in his book, a statement that deserves considerable praise.

Why is it that what we lack owns us?

Scene one: Abdulaziz, a man who has inherited great wealth that has been spent, doesn't own a house in California but he owns four houses in different cities around the world, two of which he inherited and two he bought. He feels sad for not owning a house in California and works hard throughout the year to acquire one near Santa Monica. He is not concerned about his income, which exceeds thirty thousand riyals monthly, and he doesn't want to think about anything other than finding new ways to invest as much as he can and acquire the house as soon as possible. At the same time, he doesn't want to give up his other properties.

Scene two: An athlete who won the bronze medal in the Olympics is not sad for reaching third place because he knows his name has been recorded in history as one who received a medal in one of the global events. But his teammate and competitor, who won the silver medal, still feels an overbearing sense of failure because he knows the difference between him and the gold medal was just a fraction of a second.

A Real Scene: When Pete Best was dismissed from The Beatles in the early 1960s. Initially, he was deeply saddened by this decision, feeling regretful that the band members and their manager were convinced to let him go.

However, Pete Best didn't dwell on his sadness for the rest

of his life. He eventually met his girlfriend "Cathy" (who later became his wife) and the two embarked on a long journey filled with love and harmony. Up to this day, now in his mid-seventies, they are still together.

Pete Best came to realize that his dismissal was the best thing that happened to him because, through that temporary sorrow, he managed to meet his wife and build a new and emotionally comfortable life. Mark Manson notes that Pete Best succeeded in living away from the limelight and the frenzy that accompanied the band during that time. He is grateful that his exit turned out to be one of the best things that happened in his life.

On the other hand, Dave Mustang, the singer who was fired from Metallica in 1983, sank into a state of hysteria from anger and sadness. He turned to alcohol and drugs for long periods and repeatedly tried to get revenge on the band in different ways. He obsessed over trying to outsell Metallica but failed in the attempt.

Every time he received a golden record, he saw himself as lower in status to the band that had fired him. Instead of enjoying his massive success and millions earned from concerts and song sales throughout the 80s and 90s, he was preoccupied with the question, "How can I become wealthier and more successful than Metallica?"

Mustang could have easily moved on but he chose to fight and compete in a game that was already rigged in Metallica's favour. He could have enjoyed every detail of his overwhelming success compared to other remaining singers, or perhaps he could have lived contently like Pete Best did in his life. Instead, he chose to suffer over something he didn't possess (and wouldn't ever possess).

He feels the same pain as our friend Abdulaziz in scene one.

I will later discuss how the deep desire within us always seeks more of everything, rather than focusing on what each of us possesses (in terms of possessions such as skills, time, or position). However, in the next paragraph, I will suffice with reviewing another effort that can be considered within the bounds of the "illusion of achievement" or unjustified exaggeration in the pursuit of status. This matter is related to my profession as a writer for others.

Why do I have this desire to stop reading Arabic books?

There have been many reasons that led me to almost stop reading Arabic books, particularly the local ones. The most pertinent reason among them was the obvious ulterior motives of the authors behind writing books.

I attended a quick meeting between a famous social media influencer and one of my successful entrepreneur friends. The influencer suggested that my friend should appear more on Snapchat and social media channels to share his experiences with others for marketing purposes, and maybe write a book as well. Even if the book doesn't directly relate to his field, or as he put it, "You are only missing a book."

In another scene, I was conversing with a self-improvement and training enthusiast about his desire to learn about the mechanism of writing books and content in general. I told him that the first rule of writing any attractive content is to be a frequent and immersive reader. Then comes the writing project. He replied, "Personally, I don't read. I acquire my knowledge and expertise through experiences only." I don't have an absolute objection to that but, naturally, I cannot engage in a conversation with someone who wants to discuss their writing project but is adamant about disliking reading.

The problem with the Arabic language is that the impact of the colloquial dialect and that of speaking in formal Arabic are significantly different. Unlike the English language, where books are written almost as people speak to each other, the reader feels like they are truly listening to what the writer wants to convey clearly. However, most young Arab writers are preoccupied with crafting flowery, poetic words with rhymes, neglecting the primary importance of the purpose of writing, which is conveying the truth.

Returning to the subject of intention, I notice that the task of a writer for the young Arab audience, for example, is not primarily focused on the content but rather on showcasing that the author is someone of special status.

This encouraged many to write books (without much effort) such as compiling tweets or scattered thoughts on social media pages into a text (let's call it a book). In the end, the book ends up on the shelves, and the reader does not know what topics the book covers but he might recognize the author.

When a popular fashion influencer releases a new book, it seems to me that she is trying to fill a void that didn't necessarily need to be filled. She knows herself as a "fashionista + influencer + law student"... okay!... (and now she's an author). Here, I claim that there is something wrong with the equation.

My enthusiasm for reading most Arabic books has become quite dull; they don't interest me. This is not an objection to their authors but rather due to not finding the pursuit of truth behind their writing. As Charles Bukowski put it regarding this matter, "If it doesn't come bursting out of you in spite of everything, don't do it. If you have to sit for hours staring at your computer screen or hunched over your typewriter searching for words, don't do it. If you're doing it for money or fame, don't do it. If you're doing it because you want women in your bed, don't do it. If you have to sit there and rewrite it again and again, don't do it."

And I still receive dozens of articles from friends who are followers. I don't understand what senders want to convey through their writing. They tell me this article is the beginning of a book project. But it's neither a vivid story nor a clear perspective nor topic… nor is it poetry.

My distress increases when the author communicates things that are excessively obvious. I know that waking up early is a blessing and I know that perseverance is the key to success but where is your detailed perspective on this matter? Or where can I read about your challenges and experiences with waking up early? I simply want the truth from you, without necessarily needing positive and inspiring poetic words. I do not intend to imply that I am against young people attempting to write. However, I would like to draw attention to two essential aspects regarding writing books: that writing should be done without marketing intentions for something else (like continuing the conversation about it on social media) and that the writing should aim to convey the truth through books, rather than merely painting words (as Dr. Ali AlWardi commented).

I have previously mentioned that I am against giving literary opinions on novels written by my friends, for instance. However, I always commend the search for the idea behind the work or the creative project driving it. I prefer not to wear the hat of literary critic but rather the hat of someone who encourages writing, considering the two points mentioned above.

The craft of writing remains a serious endeavor, from the commitment to start writing it to completing its design and placing it on shelves for the public. Sadly, as a regular reader, I don't feel this seriousness in Arabic books, especially the new ones. Recently, I saw an Instagram clip of a twenty-something young man informing his followers, "Finally, after five years of trying, my book is out..." It was more like a notebook or a draft of scattered thoughts he had written at different times until he decided to compile them into a small book. My issue was never with the writer as a writer... or the book. My issue arose when I followed him and found that he flooded social media channels, taking pictures at book signing platforms and with visitors to the publishing house's booth, posing alongside well-known figures holding his book. He added a comment, something along the lines of, "Finally, I published a book that will be well-received and now I have become influential in society." I wondered, "What is the book even about?... Or was it just written to increase the number of books?"

PART TWO: THE REWARD

THE REWARD AND HUMANITY

I recall that day without remembering its specific occasion when a conservative young man said to me, "I am serving you not out of love for you but seeking rewards from Allah." I felt a pricking sensation within me that I couldn't comprehend at that time. I perceived the brother to be somewhat harsh in this confession. To be fair, this incident occurred over ten years ago, with my having less awareness and greater religious apprehension.

I couldn't fathom the justification that led him to utter those words. In any case, I now remember this incident to realize that what truly bothered me was the motive behind his service, which I deemed less humane and more focused on obtaining a clear and explicit benefit —even if it remained unnoticed — from Allah, the Almighty. I assumed, perhaps controversially, that this motive (the reward) was the only one.

My question was: Is it good for him to confess this so explicitly?

What if I were not a Muslim? Would he still make such a confession? Or would circumstances, place or time prevent us from being on the same wavelength?

I analysed this situation and told myself: "If the man had served me in a different scenario, a straightforward service — assuming I were not a Muslim — it would most likely be an attempt to convince me that our religion is tolerant and perhaps his goal would be an indirect invitation for me to embrace Islam. In any case, the motive was religious and not primarily humane, as I perceived.

The Desire for Rewards

The previous incident is counteracted by another phenomenon I refer to as "the illusion of accomplishment in seeking rewards". Readers might perceive my stance on this matter negatively, knowing that I strongly oppose the dissemination of religious and preachy messages on WhatsApp and other social media channels. I am also opposed to those who send messages of unknown origin, even if they carry positive content. My issue lies in the protocol of sending, not the content itself. The reason is simple: I am completely convinced that such actions give the sender the illusion of accomplishment and undermine the importance of sources and their quality. The senders select most of those on their list and transmit supplications, prayers, educational advice or health tips consistently, convincing their subconscious minds that this act was an excellent attempt to earn rewards quickly without much effort. Copying and pasting a message and selecting a hundred people with a press of a button equals a thousand congratulations. Let your imagination calculate the reward.

Anyone unemployed can easily sit in their nightwear on the couch and send multiple daily messages to their loved ones. They turn Fridays into a time for sending preachy messages that are challenging to apply in real life.

"The illusion of accomplishment" or this type of behaviour indirectly contributes to making the senders feel an immediate sense of happiness, deluding themselves into believing that they have accomplished something deserving of praise. It is not hidden from the reader that the results of our lives do not align with this kind of action. Here are billions of messages sent to all our phones in recent years, and I realize, without attempting to justify it, that they haven't changed anything within us. Realistically, their harm outweighs their benefit. The sender does not seek permission before sending them, nor does the recipient enjoy or benefit from them most of the time. It is similar to holiday greetings messages.

Emails

At the beginning of the last millennium, precisely when email culture started spreading through society, I was naturally like any other teenager who was eager to open personal email and use it for various tasks (Hotmail Messenger was the most popular back then). After a while, I realized that this email had transformed into receiving two types of messages.

The first type, as is well known perhaps for those in my age group at the time, were messages filled with fabricated stories (like the tale of a genie in the mountain, or a woman transforming into a goat). There were also religious supplications, prayers and stories, including anything related to our heritage and spiritual culture.

These messages came from different segments of society; some were from classmates from other schools, while others were from distant relatives. Of course, many emails were from friends I met on internet chat sites and never had the chance to meet in person.

The second type of messages were the indecent ones. Almost immediately after receiving three or four religious sermons, a fifth email would come to spoil what was received.

The motive behind sending messages of the first type was "the illusion of accomplishment in obtaining rewards," while the motive behind sending messages of the second type was human.

I do not justify the second type of emails in any way but when a teenager sends such messages to a friend, the motive is surely not to seek rewards.

Teenagers know that indecent messages and silly jokes have a more realistic impact and are in line with the inner desires of youth to explore them. At the same time, I monitored my psychological behaviour at that time, when I was strongly influenced by the religious awakening period, as many teenagers were. Dealing with messages of the first type was sensitive and strange, as I didn't have the heart to delete them (thinking I might read them later and gain rewards), nor did I have the courage to politely ask the senders to refrain from sending any more messages to my email.

I vividly remember a small incident that occurred during that time in this regard. One of my friends asked another friend of ours to stop sending him preachy and advisory emails or any other copy-pasted content. The response he got from the other friend was disdainful looks that were immediately followed by the remaining members of the group expressing surprise at such a request. Their reaction was as if they were saying, "So, you don't want religious messages? That means you're bothered by religion!"

Emails have almost disappeared these days, to be replaced by new communications channels. First, there were SMS messages, then messages via Bluetooth and, eventually, WhatsApp became the dominant mode of communication.

WhatsApp

WhatsApp is arguably one of the most significant inventions to change our social dynamics. It became the family gathering, the friends' meeting place, and fundamentally replaced the old chat rooms where idle young people used to hang out. It also revolutionized romantic relationships, as young men no longer had to pay the price of expensive communications bills. Now, a voice message with a few pictures and numerous written conversations during the day costs nothing more than a Wi-Fi connection or a data package.

This ease of use put us, as one of my friends put it, at the mercy of other people's fingers. In many cases, if you don't respond to a WhatsApp message from a close person, you might face teasing. The negative feeling could escalate further when the person sees you online at the time of message delivery. Everyone is familiar with this "tax" and with the ease of use and cost-effectiveness, it's easy to invade your privacy and seize your attention at any moment.

I know some people rely solely on WhatsApp for their cultural and news information, claiming that they no longer need to read any written scientific material in books or Wikipedia. They believe that the abundance of scattered information on WhatsApp is enough to make them knowledgeable and aware of events and essential information regularly received. This belief naturally encourages them to assume that others share the same idea, leading to their continued habit of sending messages, regardless of their quality.

The attempt to refrain from receiving messages

What I wrote earlier was an introduction to what I want to draw attention to. I have been seriously trying to avoid receiving messages with unknown sources or copy/paste messages or those constantly sent by hundreds of people throughout the week. By now readers understand my level of annoyance with them.

I admit that I have a love-hate relationship with various social media channels, especially WhatsApp, primarily because of this issue.

I discovered that even if I think I can control myself after spending a lot of time on WhatsApp, in fact I still find it difficult to control my attention and not get distracted by continuously checking it.

Therefore, a few months ago, I decided to remove notifications from most apps on my mobile phone, starting with WhatsApp. If there is no need for me to see every notification during the morning because I am busy with work or writing, I prefer to spend my evenings reading something useful or being with my daughters or friends, with a higher level of mental presence. I realized that during my free time, I would still go on WhatsApp and drown in a sea of accumulated messages, most of which were neither useful nor original, but rather repetitive and copied. As a result, important messages from people I value and with whom I want to communicate were getting lost among the clutter. So, I decided to take a serious step to limit this.

I composed a general reply message to anyone sending me any kind of random messages, especially on Fridays. The text went as follows:

> *"Dear Sir/Madam,*
> *"(This is not a private message addressed to a specific person)*
> *"Peace be upon you,*
> *"I very much appreciate your eagerness to communicate with me. However, I am requesting you to exclude me from the list of Friday messages (or any other religious or social list or copy-pasted content).*
> *"Of course, this is not because I reject the content of the message, God forbid. But it is because I want to make the most of WhatsApp, which has made my work and connection with loved ones easier. I don't want these weekly messages to disrupt the quality of these communications.*
> *"I welcome you personally at any time without such messages and I welcome your words, provided they are written by you (as long as you sign your name).*
> *"Thank you for understanding."*

To my surprise, most recipients of the message were annoyed by it. One of my friends directly replied, "Why are you upset? I wanted you to earn rewards (from God)." Another responded, "I author my own messages" but the issue with the latter was that they kept resending the same message every week at the same time, which probably didn't contain any new or exceptional information. It has been the same message over and over again.

If I were to allow space for each person I have on my list to send me only one message per week, I would leave it to the reader to imagine the number of messages of wasted mental energy I would be receiving.

Through this well-organized request, I aimed to regulate the messages sent to me. I claim to be someone who loves reading, and I do indeed like to read and be informed about anything that comes into my hands. However, under one simple and obvious condition: the senders must have put effort into crafting the content of the message. They should present it to me, and their words should say, "Here, I worked on this; I hope you read it."

The situation escalated when I worked temporarily on a project that required me to communicate with dozens of people (whom I didn't know) via phone over two months. After the project concluded successfully, the unexpected morning and evening messages, as well as Friday messages, continued to flood my WhatsApp from these dozens of individuals who had saved my number. Consequently, my phone got overwhelmed with these messages, causing important messages that arrived before them, one or two days earlier, to disappear among the clutter.

One might suggest that I simply get another phone dedicated to such matters. I tried that but I don't see the need to change my daily behaviour and add another burden by carrying a second phone specifically for internet use (or for others), to be frank. And I don't believe that "the other solution" is pleasant either.

The interesting thing about this matter is that most of the

recipients of my message, requesting them to stop sending messages, continued to send them. Perhaps their motivation – if we assume good intentions – wasn't stubbornness but a clear and explicit affirmation that most of the messages were sent without consideration for the recipients or without making an extra effort to regulate the contact list. Especially when it includes people like me who do not wish to receive them, it becomes a direct response to the behaviour of copying and pasting – inconsiderate behaviour – and sending to the list regardless of the recipients' desires.

I seriously wonder if persistent senders of messages don't feel bothered when they, in turn, receive a lot of them. The equation is not clear from a behavioural perspective.

My dear friend Ahmad Hussawi has an opinion on this matter: "I believe that the continuous behaviour of sending messages, whatever their content may be, comes from a desire to maintain communication from the sender's end. It's like saying to the recipient, 'Don't forget me, I'm here despite the lack of communication and distance. Perhaps I will need you, or you will need me in the future.' While I may find this opinion worth mentioning and considering, I also find that too much of it becomes annoying rather than an attempt to maintain communication.

"Personally, I don't mind if one of the senders contacts me in the future, seeking help or assistance in a matter, even if we haven't communicated for a while. However, I do object to the repetition of sending messages."

Analysis of attempts to resolve the issue

In practise, there are several suggestions to address this problem. The easiest is to delete WhatsApp or remove social media channels altogether. However, I believe that such steps address only the surface and leave the underlying issue untouched. As a user of social media channels and WhatsApp, I have the right to enjoy them. Even if the optimal solution may be to delete them, through this book, I would be wasting the readers' time. Neither will they benefit from technological advancements nor will someone like me be able to participate in solving the problem at its core.

Here, I want to focus on the root of the problem and eliminate the cause rather than attempting to eliminate the impact.

In the future, we might encounter various forms with new communication channels. Who knows what new communication means will occupy our lives as members of this society and turn into new channels of communication.

Twitter

Writing, in general, is the easiest, best and cheapest means of self-expression. When internet users share events of their day or their opinions, they do not usually prioritize sharing them to reveal their personal lives, as some believe. They just want to express themselves.

Twitter may be the first and most sensitive place in the world to discover what lies within a person in terms of expression. Both the wealthy politician and the overworked employee find themselves there. Many repetitive preachy messages don't get repeated at the same rate simply because they will easily get lost among the heap of chitchat that will fill the timeline. If the tweet's author doesn't share a carefully crafted tweet, then no one will notice it. There won't be the same sense of accomplishment in accumulating likes and shares when targeting a more closed or private audience, like other social media channels.

On Twitter, the pursuit of rewards is replaced in a different way. Many WhatsApp senders, who may not have any harm in sending continuous religious messages, unleash different types of attacks (sometimes bigotry) in the name of religion on Twitter. It is not hidden from those familiar with Twitter that there are plenty of spontaneous responses recorded on accounts whose owners are fond of offensive language and lacking in manners. Written on their bio pages: "My Lord, have mercy on me under the earth and on the day of

'Al-Darad'. Glory be to God and praise Him, Glory be to God the Great." When it comes to any social or religious discussion, which doesn't necessarily have to be sensitive, you'll find their aggressive morale. Fortunately, one of them may have some self-control, and you'll see them attacking fiercely and injuring others, excluding explicit profanity only. But achieving this verbal battle will be enough to give them a sense of accomplishment, and perhaps, the reward.

Of course, I do not mean, in everything mentioned in this chapter, the owners of fake and unknown accounts. Those are a different matter.

Reward means reciprocation

In our upbringing and culture, a person cannot feel a sense of accomplishment without a clear and explicit return. Most people do not praise God because He is deserving of praise, but rather with the primary goal of obtaining compensation. Regardless of the superficial ways of obtaining compensation.

I believe almost firmly that if there were no authentic Prophetic traditions about the reward of praising God, for example, you wouldn't find many people doing it.

Please don't misunderstand me; I'm not against remembrance (*dhikr*) – of course not. However, I am against the sole motivation that drives our behaviour, which has reflected on us. The only reason many of us write *dhikr* on our bios is to unconsciously ensure that the page visitors will read these *dhikr* and thus share the reward with them.

Personally, I don't think it's appropriate to mention God in this manner, and it's not fitting for His greatness to be mentioned in accordance with our old culture that encouraged sending messages to dozens of your friends, which I'm grateful has disappeared without a return.

The phenomenon of writing *dhikr* on bios is comparable to the sent messages on various remaining communication channels. It reinforces, even if slightly or unconsciously, the tendency to avoid real work and distract the individual from oneself a little and from the work that should occupy them, as human behaviour stems from thoughts that motivate them, a mix of their conscious and unconscious mind and old programming they grew up with. Maybe the impact of the old school of thought that emphasized making others read *dhikr* (even if it's done without realizing its greatness) would make them feel responsible to fulfill their duty and thus create attempts to flatten things out, like writing *dhikr* on bios as if it acts as a "collective reward box" for everyone, thus achieving a clear "illusion of accomplishment".

Furthermore, this pattern of thinking might subconsciously lead a person to continue searching for simple channels with a continuous reward, which do not require effective efforts for others, thus focusing on writing *dhikr* wherever they put their name on different accounts.

The effort is less when continuously writing and sending *dhikr* or including it in the bio. The fatigue is greater when working on researching something, providing valuable information, or real values to benefit others to share. Writing *dhikr* might be more enticing from the perspective of rewards, which cannot be guaranteed from other worldly matters using the same line of thinking.

And finally, as long as there is a return, there will be continuity. Some people will continue writing in their bio, "Editor, Palestine," and "Rocket Engineer", along with many other things they want to define themselves through, if it's not a clear and direct introduction or if religious *dhikr* is not mentioned in it.

The Collective Mind

The collective mind, undoubtedly, is always unconscious but this unconsciousness might be one of the secrets of its power. In the natural world, creatures that are largely governed by their instincts accomplish astonishingly complex tasks that may amaze us. The role played by the unconscious in all our actions is immense and the conscious mind's role is very small. Unconscious actions are like a force that is still unknown.

Here, Gustave Le Bon attempts to analyze the collective mind (or public behaviour) by examining unconscious behaviours that, when combined, form the behaviour that manifests in reality. While I don't seriously claim that Le Bon has reached a definitive answer to his questions in this regard, recognizing the existence of repetitive unconscious behaviours may be the first step in understanding the human psyche.[7]

Le Bon argues about the idea that the collective mind or general mindset of people is often similar in their beliefs and when it comes to personal perspectives, even if they differ greatly in intellectual convictions. He comments on

---

7   This was one of the most important issues in the lives and works of prominent figures like Carl Jung and Sigmund Freud, who later addressed human "unconscious" behaviours after Gustave Le Bon's time. And I firmly believe that if they had the opportunity to meet Le Bon, humanity would have been influenced by his exceptional works, for God has wisdom in everything.

this: "Humans are extremely diverse in their instinctive intelligence and passion, yet very similar in everything related to the realm of emotions, such as religion, politics, ethics, emotions, and hatred, and so on."

Rarely do prominent individuals (or evolved ones) surpass the level of most ordinary individuals in this similarity. From an intellectual standpoint, there might be a vast difference between a great mathematician and a manual labourer but from a personal perspective, the difference is often minimal or non-existent and these general characteristics exist in the persona of the collective mind. It's governed by the unconscious and is within the behaviour of the majority of ordinary individuals at the same level, and I say that crowd behaviour has become a communal process. In the collective mind, individuals' intellectual capabilities weaken, thus compromising their individual independence.

Here, we might find, despite the vast differences between two personalities, one successful, evolved and educated, and the other simple and limited in mentality, they engage in many similar behaviours to fulfill their inner emotional needs (such as sending preachy messages).

It might not be logical for us to express surprise in this matter that represents the concept of the "collective mind". You find the intellectually advanced doctor and the simple employee both encouraging a union club, and repeatedly sending messages on WhatsApp, all in order to satisfy their needs and apply emotional convictions for themselves.

The pursuit of achievement, self-enhancement, or seeking compensation significantly falls within the framework of the personal (emotional) collective mind. The advanced individual we mentioned may clearly know the principles that make them more successful and developed in their work and professional or intellectual life, but this clarity may not be evident in emotional achievements, like seeking compensation, for instance.

It is not surprising to see a top hospital or bank manager consistently engaging in behaviours such as sending preachy messages or popular videos to their friends and family along with "good morning" and "good evening" images. These individuals are advanced and have a thoughtful approach in their profession and position only, but they are similar to the general public in emotional matters (and aspirations).

Understanding human behaviour and distinguishing between emotion and reason is one of the most important aspects through which we can comprehend the hidden drivers behind our actions. With this awareness, we can then make independent decisions towards achieving genuinely valuable objectives.

Unfortunately, emotion often dominates our attitudes and actions. Here arises a logical question: What results would we achieve in our lives if we surrendered all our actions to emotion and removed the "filter" of reason?

"The public possesses, in their ordinary qualities, what explains why they can never accomplish tasks that require a high degree of intelligence." Le Bon comments, "In the public, all emotions and actions are contagious, to the extent that individuals are willing to sacrifice their private interests for the public interest. This ability contradicts the individual's personal nature, which is difficult to overcome, except when they become a part of the public."

From this, we understand that attempts to seek compensation in any way are just a repetition of what others do, whether they are convinced or not.

Professional types of works that require a high degree of intelligence cannot be performed simultaneously by all members of the public. Why? Because the difficulty lies in the fact that actions or behaviours characterized by quality or high levels of intelligence may not be acceptable to individuals who are not intelligent unless they are an integral part of the collective behaviour.

This explains another important point: that intelligence alone may not be sufficient. For an individual to progress, they may need to draw on some courage to engage in smart actions that may not be socially acceptable.

So, any intelligent and daring step in one's professional or practical life may not be carried out by the individual because it is not well-received by society, unlike superficial behaviours performed by many simply because they are socially acceptable, or as the common saying goes, "the majority prevails".

This encourages safer actions that emotionally resonate with everyone. Even if someone reaches a high level of intelligence and lacks some bravery, they may not dare to present social or religious analyses in front of the public, and it is safer for them to be like everyone else. Even if it doesn't require any pause or reflection on its value. On the other hand, if an individual uses different creative means and methods, they may face not direct rejection but disapproval at the very least. Why? Because their actions differ from the well-known collective behaviour.

How many highly intelligent individuals do you know with few exceptional achievements? I'm sure the reader knows many from this category. With a little analysis, you may find that the condition of such individuals is a result of their lack of courage to attempt to apply what their mind constantly suggests, or a lack of mental resilience to withstand the shocks and differences they experienced in previous situations or periods in front of others.

The Story of the Land

Years ago, I went out with my father one day heading to some event, and the route required passing through a back street near our house. My father asked me to stop for a moment next to an empty plot of land and said, "Look at this land, how wonderful it is, with three streets surrounding it. It's perfect for a large building. The location is excellent." After contemplating it for a while, we continued on our way.

During the journey, my father was occupied with imagining various scenarios about the land – what could be built on it in detail, how he could plan to acquire it or collaborate on a project with someone. He continued this imaginative exercise for several weeks. His motivation was partly due to the overcrowding of the neighbourhood. He also knew that the existing buildings in the area did not meet the demand and were poorly constructed by most contractors.

He told me that this land could easily accommodate a residential building with at least twenty apartments and a villa on the roof. More than twenty families could have lived there. And of course, this imagination presented a long-term investment opportunity.

After several months, I had to pass by that land on my way to some errand, only to find that it had been sold and entirely allocated for building a mosque.

The mosque was built within a few months with

luxury construction, amid the congested non-luxury neighbourhood.

Before making any negative comments, I must clarify that our area already had three mosques, with the farthest being no more than a ten-minute walk away.

The last of those mosques had recently been renovated and was no less luxurious than the mosque mentioned. In fact, it was large enough to barely fill up during Friday prayers (it could accommodate around three thousand worshippers, men and women, if my estimation is correct). It was well-managed and had many activities.

After the construction of the last mosque, I noticed a large sign hanging on its door, stating that it was donated by one of the wealthier individuals. I took some time to calculate the cost of this mosque over the next ten years after its establishment and I found that, without exaggeration, its total costs would easily exceed ten million riyals, including the value of the land. The residents of the neighbourhood, including myself, knew that this mosque was not the best project to serve their needs, given the presence of several nearby mosques, one of which already surpassed its capacity.

I am not well-versed in the management of mosques but, based on the information I have, their administration is usually entrusted to one of the relevant ministries. In such cases, the project director or the donor building the mosque may not have regular and close supervision of its management, unlike what might happen if the land were used for a charitable building, such as housing for newly-weds or those in need. Such a project would possibly require more hands-on involvement.

I found that the construction of that mosque, with a

simple analysis, seemed to be an attempt to distance oneself from the real work that would serve the community in a fundamental way. In my view, housing remains a priority, especially when there is no shortage of mosques.

I believe the donor had his intentions, seeking reward from Allah with a noble purpose, considering the number of worshippers during the five daily prayers, which perhaps motivated him to overlook the community's needs, even if they were charitable. The concept of reward, in terms of numbers, is often more appealing than the worldly benefit, as housing is limited while worshippers are diverse and continuous.

Real Work in people

I read about a young woman recounting her father's will before his passing. He requested that a portion of his inheritance be donated to educate some young people aspiring to continue their studies. The young woman, as she claimed, supervised one of the students from his graduation through medical school until he completed his studies and began working. Through his work, he was able to treat both Muslims and non-Muslims alike. Perhaps, and I am aware of this possibility, this act of kindness might extend further, encouraging the doctor to provide free treatment to some of his patients or oversee the education of others once his financial situation improves in the future. The cycle of goodness continues, as it is the foundation of the human instinct in dealing with others.

This leads me to a question that naturally arises: How many students could have been educated with those ten million riyals over ten years? And would the true value, from a humanitarian and religious perspective, have had the same impact as the mosque in question? Allah knows best.

Breaking the fast for a wealthy person

During Ramadan, years ago, I stopped a few minutes before Maghrib prayer at a traffic light in one of the luxury neighbourhoods of Jeddah, on my way to another district. On my right was a Bentley car, and on the other side, there was a Lexus Jeep. Within seconds, a group of kind-hearted young men passed by, offering us a small meal (dates, yogurt, water, and snacks), intending to earn the reward of breaking a fast for a fasting person on the road. I insisted on not accepting the meal because I was heading to my home, like most Saudi households, where a large iftar feast awaited. The young man insisted on giving me the bag of food after a quick exchange, trying to earn the reward rather than any monetary compensation. He succeeded in doing the same with the drivers of the other two cars.

Afterwards, I reproached myself for not accepting the meal, which would undoubtedly have been valuable to someone in need elsewhere in the country. As a joke, I told myself that the arrangement of food at home (dates, then soup, then samosas, for example) that I had in mind would be disrupted after accepting that meal. There were plenty of choices.

Most likely, the owners of the Bentley and the Lexus at the traffic light were wealthier than the young men distributing the meals, and they certainly did not need the charity of a meal bag.

At the same time in Ramadan, years ago, I saw, on Tahlia Street (another luxury street in Jeddah), one of the young men I knew distributing iftar meals to pedestrians at the traffic light.

I happily informed my friends that I saw so-and-so distributing iftar meals on that street. To that, a unified chorus of voices replied, "Oh, that guy is known for constantly trying to flirt with girls." There was no better place than Tahlia for them to laugh at the idea.

The response shocked me, and I told them that so-and-so was better than them in his efforts to provide iftar to fasting people, while they were lazy, sitting around drinking coffee, not doing anything since they returned from work during the day. One of them replied, criticizing the person distributing iftar, saying, "So-and-so has a family and two children from his previous marriage. It would have been better for him to spend all those iftar meals in Jeddah to see the poor and destitute and give them iftar there. Or it would have been better for him to sit with his family and children."

After that, a heated discussion ensued in the gathering about whether what the young man was doing was right or not. Everyone agreed that the humanitarian value of providing iftar to a fasting person is equivalent to the reward promised by Allah. The difference of opinion was about the method of distributing iftar, not the principle. This led me to side with the latter opinion. The young men in Tahlia and Al-Khalediya seemed determined to fulfill the meaning of "breaking a fast for a fasting person" regardless of whether the person was genuinely fasting or in dire need of iftar. Any simple Muslim knows that the essence of fasting is to feel the deprivation experienced by the poor, and thus encourage dealing with them through charitable acts, including providing iftar during the holy month of Ramadan.

The effort of these young men, who took time and exerted effort from their lives to provide iftar for others, remains commendable. However, it raises a question: Why didn't they go to places or people who were more in need of that iftar than those present at those locations? Is it because this task was slightly more challenging and required additional real work?

My opinion tends to align with the rational approach, as mentioned earlier. I have experienced and continue to experience a small situation where I do not benefit from the iftar meal offered to me in the middle of the street (except in very exceptional cases). Perhaps, I find myself more inclined to focus on real and exhausting work, by dedicating time, money and effort to serve those in need in their own locations or through official channels with the government. Not in Tahlia or Al-Khalediya, where most of the residents or passersby are not in need of charity.

On a narrower scale, regarding Jeddah, for example, most of the simple porters and other needy individuals are better accommodated in mosques and many other official charitable channels, purely for the chance of receiving a free iftar. They certainly do not roam around in Tahlia and Al-Khalediya to meet young people in order to get an iftar meal.

Human intellect, time and effort are limited and my attempt to address what has been mentioned is nothing more than a discussion of an idea, to direct that time and effort to their proper place. The more a person engages in activities without questioning whether they truly have a direct and genuine impact, the more they will experience an "illusion of achievement" that is never fulfilled.

I am not here to evaluate the actions of others, as every individual is free in any case. However, I wanted to draw attention to the fact that directing mental energies before physical and temporal ones is more appropriate and it will yield remarkable effects, even if they are intangible at that moment. If we gather and replace all the time spent copying and sending repetitive messages with a single call to a friend, offering assistance in solving their work-related problem, that would undoubtedly be a genuine action that propels society forward.

Similarly, if everyone replaced their generic social media bios with a more specific introduction like "I work in the field of X, how can I help you?" the impact of those words would be much greater on others.

Despite all this, the overwhelming majority still tends to gravitate towards easier tasks that do not require any additional effort.

And the question arises again, why does this happen?

I say that humans respond psychologically to the sense of accomplishment rather than the actual result. Just like a manager who fires one of his employees due to poor performance and results, and the employee responds by saying that he is working hard and showing up to work daily, believing that he has done what is required.

The employee's sense of achievement and the accomplished employee (after leaving a job)

In response to the last example, I would like to clarify that one of the worst moments for a manager, for instance, is when one of his accomplished employees submits their resignation. The manager will try hard to retain them by offering additional salary, commissions or any other incentives to keep them. Simply because he does not want to let them go as the workplace has become better with their presence since the employee contributes with real work and the manager will find it very difficult to continue the work without them. This is in contrast to the other employee who believes that they have accomplished their duties just by showing up and leaving, with the feeling that they are tired of hard work.

Real work and true value lie in consistency amid the chaos of emotions.

I often come across heated debates when acquaintances leave their jobs, regardless of the reasons. The latest of these debates was when a woman posted on social media that she left her job, politely stating that it was due to financial challenges the company was facing. I saw a group of friends encouraging her to take legal steps to demand additional compensation or severance pay for leaving.

Their encouragement was merely an attempt to offer moral support, and this perhaps reflects the prevailing belief in society that all companies and businesses are oppressors and possess excessive money that deserves to be taken by any means, even if it's through cunning intentions without legitimate grounds. I know dozens of stories of friends who quit their jobs and then went on a quest with government authorities to demand compensation from their former employers who had let them go.

Here, I want to emphasize that everyone should seek their rights if they deserve them. However, I mean seeking rights in an objective manner, not based on feelings or the belief that it is an absolute and rightful entitlement. It wasn't necessarily natural for companies to let go of employees if they were already performing well and going above and beyond the basic requirements (assuming the financial situation of the company is not too dire). Exceptional employees probably wouldn't be occupied with demanding compensation. Instead, they would be focusing on their immediate future and upcoming opportunities, as those are likely to present themselves immediately after leaving the job. Ultimately, only the truth prevails.

Furthermore, I would like to add that focusing on the bigger and more critical picture, concentrating on skills, accomplishing real work and producing actual results remain more essential. No matter how much employees have the ability to claim their rights through negotiations or by force, such action would remain a temporary achievement that does not directly serve their future. In such cases, I suggest dedicating the least amount of mental focus, time and effort to demanding rights if they exist and allocating the majority of effort to engage in what is more important: developing current skills and striving for accomplishments and working towards the next steps in life.

PART 3:
THE IMPACT

THE EGO AND LEAVING AN IMPACT

Try asking a group of Saudi (or perhaps Gulf) university girls about the names of five ministers who served in Saudi Arabia or the Gulf countries during the past decades, and I bet most of them will mention the name of the late Minister Ghazi Al Qusaibi among the five.

Is it because he was the best or most successful minister? Or is it because he left an impact on others through his writings and stances?

I discussed this important question with my dear friend Ayman Jamal (the producer of the film "Bilal"). What did he try to achieve through his strenuous work in producing that film? Was it success? And if so, how is that success measured? By profit or by fame?

The discussion led us to the idea that the goal of "leaving an impact" is what he said he was trying to achieve through producing that film.

People are automatically driven to pursue success in their lives, despite the vast differences in how each person defines success. Some see it as giving their children the best education, while others view it as buying a specific house or car within a certain period of life. Furthermore, many define success through acquiring an educational degree of some sort. It goes without saying that most of us live with the ambition to achieve a number of accomplishments probably similar to those mentioned, and we hold on to them until some or all of them are realized.

The concept of success and its understanding, from my perspective, is always linked to a specific time and scope. If a person says, "I want to earn a certain amount of money within a particular time frame", this is a specific measure of financial success. If they achieve this goal within the desired time, they have undoubtedly succeeded in it and will move on to another goal to strive for further success. Life moves on with small successes and one then day society decides to label the person "a successful individual".

As a person advances in age and in their professional life, new wish lists for achievements are projected. If owning a certain house was the measure of success for a specific period, then owning another house will likely be the aim for the following period. And if they achieve that second house, the definition of success might be transformed to include a new type of aspiration, like desiring to write a book at that stage of their life.

The scope of success, in my assessment, also depends on the individual. If a friend of mine is mainly concerned about obtaining a doctoral degree, it might not mean the same to me as a self-employed person and regular writer. In some cases, under extreme circumstances, another person might find that obtaining a doctoral degree is a waste of valuable time that could have been spent on something else they consider more important from their perspective. Every person is free to choose their path and what they believe serves their best interests since aspirations and priorities vary greatly with each person and situation.

A quick look at our surroundings would truly reveal that the concept of success and its magnitude indeed vary significantly depending on circumstances. For example, there is a vast difference between the concept of future success of a young man who recently inherited a decent amount of money compared to the concept of success of a self-made or beginner young person in their career.

Going back to my discussion with Ayman, he told me that his film, which he worked on for years, was the result of the impact left on him by the late director Moustafa Al Aqqad (the director of the films "The Message" and "Omar Al Mukhtar"). Here, we are talking about another concept of success, one that can be described as a new concept of authentic work that leaves an impact.

Success and Leaving an impact

Success can be measured based on following points:

1. Success can be measured by a specific time, magnitude and situation
2. Successes end with the person's life along with their achievements
3. Success is related to the self or the ego before it is related to others

It could be said that leaving an impact may happen through the following criteria:

1. Leaving an impact changes the lives of others before benefiting us directly
2. The impact cannot be precisely measured but it can be felt
3. Leaving an impact is not contingent upon time limits
4. Leaving an impact is not usually contained within a specific scope
5. The impact continues even after the person's death.

Here I find that the Prophet Muhammad, peace be upon him, had set the highest example of leaving an impact through simplicity. Every Muslim knows that he did not live a life of luxury nor did he accumulate short-term possessions during his lifetime. Instead, he was occupied with leaving an impact and conveying the message of Islam until his passing. We now see more than a billion Muslims living based on the impact left by his message.

The difficulty of leaving an impact lies in the unpredictability of its results, as it is impossible to be sure of them from the beginning. Its success and influence on others cannot be measured, which creates uncertainty in whether it will necessarily contribute to changing their lives or not.

Examples of Leaving an Impact

Some might say that success can be associated with leaving an impact. If we succeed in earning a lot of money, doesn't this result affect those around us by giving them a better life through financial support? Doesn't that count as leaving an impact? Here, of course, I could nod in agreement to this question but when I tried to differentiate between the concept of success and leaving an impact, I wanted to draw attention to the fact that the impact I'm referring to is about leaving an impact on a larger percentage of society, or more accurately, on a broader circle beyond our personal sphere.

Writing an insightful book that you've put effort into, or crafting a novel through which you attempt to influence the reader's imagination and emotions, is considered leaving an impact.

Establishing sustainable charitable initiatives is considered leaving an impact.

Creating films with powerful messages is considered leaving an impact.

Creating paintings that have exhilarated the artist's imagination to convey a deep idea or concept is considered leaving an impact.

Participating in scientific research that might change people's lives is a genuine attempt to leave an impact.

Notice that all these examples, if successfully carried out, will continue to have an effect for decades or even centuries after the creator's passing. Even if they touch only specific individuals, they will have achieved their purpose.

Our Lives and Leaving an impact

I find it fair and acceptable to devote a person's life goals between attempts to achieve personal achievements and attempts to leave a legacy.

Personally, I strive to achieve personal and material success through my daily work (for which I receive a salary) and through investing in conventional projects and other channels, as many do, with the possibility of achieving success or not.

In any case, I live each day with the intention to get closer to a particular success to achieve it. Once one success is achieved, I instinctively aim for another.

Regarding leaving an impact, I have chosen the profession of writing as the means through which I hope to leave an impact on anyone in this world.

Since 2014, I have made it known to others that "I write" and have avoided mentioning other aspects of my life. Each time I mention writing, I try to gauge the recipients interest in my profession, as there may be an opportunity for them to give their time and attention to my writings, which might potentially influence them in some way.

There is nothing wrong with focusing on material or social successes without necessarily trying to leave an impact on a broader circle of people. For example, striving for better financial returns for a dignified life, marriage or the future of one's children is a noble goal and a genuine endeavour that will reflect on us and those close to us. It's important to note here that I mentioned attempting to accomplish real work for the self, not merely convincing oneself of an accomplishment that gives a false sense of achievement.

The desire to achieve rewards (as discussed in part two in this book) is linked to leaving a legacy but only if it is employed in the right way. It cannot be achieved through the illusion of achievement. True success is achieved by obtaining higher income, gaining better knowledge or actively participating in society. It is not achieved by simply telling others that we will do something or through posting pictures that we have already done it.

The true value and real achievements often differ from what appears publicly.

If, somehow, I managed to indirectly convince others that I have tens of millions of riyals in my bank account, it wouldn't necessarily mean that I actually possess that amount in reality. Similarly, sharing dozens of pictures from workshops or seminars does not automatically indicate that I have genuinely benefited from them or that I successfully applied the knowledge to myself or others. We should collectively comprehend this inherent and strange distinction.

We need to realize that pictures do not necessarily reflect our reality, which we fully understand within ourselves.

In general, the concept of leaving an impact or creating a legacy is simple, deep and at the same time challenging to achieve. I will dedicate a section of this book to delve into it more thoroughly.

LEAVING AN IMPACT THROUGH WORK

In 1922, in the Swiss canton of St. Gallen near the southern banks of Lake Zurich, there was a small village called Bollingen. Renowned psychiatrist Carl Gustav Jung chose this spot to be his retreat from the world.

He started his life there in a small house he called "The Tower" after returning from a trip to India, where he discovered the significance of allocating rooms in a home dedicated for meditation. To accommodate this new conviction, he designated an office space for himself instead of a typical living room, by choosing that small house.

"In the solitude of my room, I am completely isolated," says Jung, describing his small room that occupies most of the house's space. "I alone possess the key to that house; I give it no one no matter what and no one can enter it without my permission," he adds.

Journalist Mason Curry, in his book "Daily Rituals", describes the work habits of the famous psychologist, mentioning that Jung's schedule was to wake up at 7 AM and, after a hefty breakfast, work uninterrupted for two hours. He spent most of the noon hours in contemplation and reflection or investing some time walking around the building. He continues to work during the evenings and, when necessary, spent the night there even though the house has no electricity. An oil lamp provided illumination.

Jung's day ended with him going to bed around 10 pm. "The feeling I experienced through renewal and contemplation there was profound from the beginning," Jung comments.

Best-selling author Cal Newport remarks on this matter, "To some, it might seem that the small house he purchased was meant for vacations, but by observing his life, one would discover that Jung could not afford to take a break from his work at that time. A year before (in 1921), he had published one of his most important books, "Psychological Types", which solidified the many fundamental differences between him and his dear friend and teacher, Sigmund Freud."

Differing with someone of Freud's stature and knowledge, the most famous psychologist of the time, was an incredibly bold step. To support his book which was released at that time, and his other works that presented his disagreement with his teacher, Jung had to remain alert and focused to systematically produce countless articles and various other books that would reinforce his innovative psychological school, "Analytical Psychology", and his dissent from Freud.

Newport adds, "Jung worked as a lecturer and a psychological counsellor, keeping him occupied most of the time. However, he was not satisfied with this preoccupation alone. Through his research and works, he aimed to change people's understanding of the 'unconscious mind'. To succeed in this mission, he had to be engrossed in deeper and more concentrated work than the prevailing lifestyle in the bustling city of Zurich.

"For Jung, his resorting to the village of Bollingen was not about escape from his professional work but rather to elevate himself to an entirely new level."

Carl Jung is considered one of the most important thinkers of the twentieth century. His theories have contributed to psychologically transforming people's lives in ways that some ordinary observers and non-specialists in human psychology may not fully grasp. His theories explained many patterns of human behaviour that were not known before.

He identified two primary personality types in humans: the extrovert or social, and the introvert or non-social. Societies used to overlook one of the most fundamental psychological differences among their individuals, often believing that a person who is non-social, for example, suffers from a pathological condition that requires treatment. However, Jung's research and findings informed us that individuals with non-social personalities do not suffer from any psychological defects; instead, it is just a natural variation in personalities. Advanced societies in the world now deal intuitively with this difference and reputable profit-oriented institutions, for instance, won't encourage their non-social employees to work in positions that require frequent interactions with others.

His works also contributed to addressing many other sensitive topics, including the significance of dreams in our lives, which reflect the contents of our subconscious minds. In fact, one issue of "National Geographic" magazine ranked Jung's differences with his teacher Freud and the works that resulted from it, "On the Unconscious Mind", as one of the top 100 discoveries in human history.

Carl Jung and Deep Work

Jung was forty-seven years old (in the year 1922) when he embarked on his new work habits, which were also a reflection of his significant divergence from his mentor. Following the publication of his book, which acted as a spark for this divergence, he went on to release a series of scientific books and articles that reshaped the field of psychology, exerting a substantial influence on the outcomes we have today. Not to mention his dissatisfaction with spending most of his working hours giving lectures and tending to his patients only, he wanted more. He wanted to create impact, leave a legacy.

His other issue was that he wasn't wealthy enough to encourage him to retire and dedicate his days extensively to his research and intellectual pursuits.

Jung's financial circumstances necessitated that he remained a faculty member and earn his livelihood by seeing patients. Yet, these two activities were somewhat of an "illusion of accomplishment" in his eyes – either just performing traditional and limited work every day, much like any other conventional doctor.

During that period, one might also find that the Swiss scientific community included evening clubs that brought together thinkers, writers and scientists. These social gatherings led to his strong friendship with his fellow countryman Einstein.

If he were to socially withdraw from those scientific clubs, it would have been a personal and academic loss for him. His continuous presence was an essential component in elevating his scientific work in various ways. Perhaps he couldn't achieve exceptional scientific breakthroughs without this daily aspect of his life.

Just as the gatherings and meetings of writers and authors during that period (1919-1939) in Paris played a regular and systematic role, with figures like Ernest Hemingway, John Paul Sartre, Colette, George Orwell, James Joyce and others, producing exceptional, impactful and timeless literary works, there was another side in Zurich. In specific, its meetings and gatherings.

Notably, both literary colleagues in Paris (Hemingway and Jean-Paul Sartre) received Nobel Prizes. The writer Jeff Jones argues that the regular convergence of these authors in a single environment had a profound contribution in making their literary productions exceptional.[8]

Jung spent the years between the age of forty-seven and his passing at the age of eighty-five within the framework of his innovative routine. Early mornings were dedicated to tasks that required more concentration and thinking. Afternoons and evenings were spent seeing patients and giving lessons. He allocated his evenings and pre-sleep hours to professional meetings at clubs, in addition to his personal matters.

From a technical perspective, this change was a somewhat

---

8 One intriguing story involves the writer Jean-Paul Sartre, who declined the Nobel Prize in 1964, offering the explanation: "There is a difference between writing my name Jean-Paul Sartre and writing Jean-Paul Sartre, Nobel Prize winner in literature. A writer must not allow himself to be turned into an institution, even if it takes a large share of the honour."

modest change in his daily schedule, dedicating less than four hours to deep work that required extensive thinking and focus (without interruptions), leaving the rest of the day for other tasks.

Most of his productivity came during the last thirty years of his life. Looking at it from another angle, most of his productivity happened during the newly allocated three hours in his daily schedule for deep work.

Personally, I don't bet that Jung possessed exceptional intelligence or a special ability beyond that of an average person or a discerning reader (who also has twenty-four hours in a day), and similarly to other psychoanalysts, he had numerous daily tasks to attend to, with the number of patients potentially increasing. Plus, he had a substantial amount of social and non-social commitments.

What Jung did was allocate time, attention and mental effort – only three hours, if the account is accurate.

With the commitment to allocate and maintain these three hours for a sustained period of time and without interruption, he changed history.

The other version of Jung is a psychologist working in some city in 2018, seeing dozens of patients every day until he fully retires. He becomes occupied with new goals in his life afterward, not necessarily professional goals, but those that aim to leave some kind of impact.

Jung's divergence from Freud happened after he presented his ideas that challenged the logic of Freud's school (analytical psychology). These ideas were valid and accurate but Jung would remain at the mercy of Freud's opinions if he didn't substantiate his differences and new ideas with compelling arguments. Moreover, the scientific community would likely criticize him if he didn't support his new ideas, which would naturally be rejected if not backed by solid scientific support. Here, one could argue that Jung chose to support his ideas scientifically before seeking social support through his colleagues' involvement. Social support might fade or harbor hidden sentiments but the impact of real work endures for a long time.

Such a scenario of divergence can be seen in many contexts, situations and different types of works during these times. Unfortunately, most people don't often dedicate time and effort to deep work that could potentially lead to them saying, "I differ from my professor and here are the results and evidence of my divergence" or "this is a meticulously worked-upon piece, please give it some attention". Most of us are preoccupied with accepting information, messages and ideas without any debate, scepticism, or even suggesting new opportunities for discussion. This is what is realistically referred to as "programming". The general mind is programmed, likely influenced by media, schooling, social environment and, of course, the emphasis on seeking social status over producing sturdy works and impacts on ourselves and our surroundings.

Using this example, I've talked about dedicating time, effort and mental focus, not about exceptional genius.

The problem of the economy and modern society

The problem of the economy and modern society (and its circumstances) is that they continue to drive people towards the superficiality in which we live. This superficiality has given rise to a large set of behaviours characterized by shallow work and its consequential influence but which is not entirely unbeneficial.

The presence of emails, social communications and technological advancements might momentarily convince us that we possess better circumstances that do not necessitate delving into the concept of deep work. Information has become more accessible and communications has become ten times easier compared to 1922. However, I find this evolution has directly contributed to impacting our way of life, where true initiatives and meaningful endeavours that bring about change often get overshadowed by the multitude of emails, decentralized meetings and social media posts that don't add much value to us or others.

Modern media always portrays the best individuals, making you feel at times that you can become like them or even better, due to their frequent appearances. It saddens me to say that if you were to conduct a quick search in any field where you aim to excel or achieve, you will almost always find someone better, faster or with lower costs.

Do you want to read more books? There are thousands

who read multiple times what you read in a year. Do you want to become a better graphic designer? There are thousands more creative than you, with a higher willingness to serve others at lower prices than you. Do you want to be a better writer? Oh, what a long journey that is. The ease with which media and modern economy depict those who have reached the pinnacle of success in their fields might be flawed by not delving into the minutiae of their daily lives, habits and routines. This could make everyone easily dismiss the boundless challenge by showcasing only what can be displayed through social media channels, attempting to condense the journey in the pursuit of self-achievement and seeking approval from others.

So, what's the solution?

– Work to leave an impact on others and our surroundings through deep and continuous work, and do it in a subtle and quiet way

– Seek happiness in what we do instead of showing others that we are happy

– Focus on steering clear of quick gains and shortcuts

Quick gains

The author Cal Newport explains in his book "Deep Work" that we have entered an era where the fast-paced economy demands a specific quality of work: deep work. This is work that requires more thinking and effort throughout the day to achieve exceptional results over an extended period of time. For example, Einstein focused on his research before presenting the theory of relativity and Steve Jobs crafted Apple's products, along with other authors who devoted their lives to create novels or books that left a mark on human history, immortalizing their names along with them. This is precisely the opposite of what the general population does. Unfortunately, this type of lengthy and profound work does not motivate them.

An investor in the stock market can achieve exceptional success only if they invest more time and effort in seeking and meticulously studying opportunities to make informed decisions on where and how to invest. An example of this is the renowned investor Warren Buffett, the "value" investor, who reads more than five hundred pages of financial reports daily and delves deeply into companies' details. Similarly, the late Abdulrahman Al-Sumait spent most of his life in Africa, dedicating himself to impactful work that served the poor and promoted Islam through actions and efforts, far from sending daily messages on WhatsApp to friends.

You can see that laziness or seeking shortcuts are the

primary enemies of deep work, true work and creative work.

Cal Newport defines his concept of "deep work" as:

"Deep work is professional activities performed in a state of distraction-free concentration that push your cognitive capabilities to their limit. These efforts create new value, improve your skill, and are hard to replicate or replace at a professional level."

In a way, this definition is precisely the opposite to what I termed as "the illusion of achievement", where individuals engage in various scattered tasks that do not produce real value for them or their environment, nor necessarily develop a specific skill or advance their professional level. This state can be applied to our professional work and personal behaviours in the pursuit of compensation, social status and other personal matters.

Newport adds, "I coined the term 'deep work' myself and while Carl Jung did not apply this at first, his work practices and behaviours at that time came from a person who understood what deep work means, and he went further to apply it at a later time."

He follows up by quoting the journalist Mason Currey, "Jung's stay at Bollingen Tower took time away from extensive responsibilities and reduced the time he spent doing hospital consultation visits which had been constant but he did not hesitate to allocate time for deep work and research. Newport adds, "Carl Jung's deep work was necessary to change the world."

If you study the lives of the most inspiring people in modern history, you will certainly find that there is a shared approach among them, Newport says, adding, "The philosopher Michel de Montaigne in the sixteenth century was deeply engaged in his work in his tower at Chateau de Montaigne in southern France, and the renowned writer Mark Twain wrote The Adventures of Tom Sawyer on Quarry Farm in New York, where he spent his summers. Twain's intense focus sometimes led him to forget to eat."

Woody Allen

As we approach modern history, we find the screenwriter and director Woody Allen has written and directed forty-nine films during the span of over six decades of his professional life since the early 1960's. Twenty-four of these films have received Academy Award nominations. Allen wrote the screenplays for all of these films not on a personal computer but using an old typewriter given to him in the 1950s. This may be one of the main reasons that made him extremely productive and disciplined by staying away (which is difficult for me and my generation's children) from social media channels and traditional communications tools. This directly contributed to producing valuable works that will continue to endure for decades to come.

What intrigues me about Woody Allen's life is that he never considers himself obsessed with strenuous work (in fact, he is technically considered lazy). He enjoys entertaining himself by watching baseball games and is a member of a jazz band that regularly performs on a weekly basis. In other words, he loves entertainment – perhaps more than me and the readers. It's noteworthy that this man, who has passed the age of eighty as I write these lines, is still at the same level of productivity and creativity as when he entered this industry over forty-five years ago.

What's even more fascinating about his lifestyle is that he doesn't work long hours during the day on his writings and films. He explains this in one of his interviews: "If you commit to working for three to five hours during the day, you will be extremely productive. It's the continuity that counts (not the strenuous work). Sitting at the typewriter every day is what makes you a productive person."

Newport's notes on the life of the director most distant from the achievement illusion are summarized in his statement: "At the beginning of his career, Woody Allen identified what works were most rewarding and valuable for his time and effort, so he focused firmly on them, moving further away from superficial matters that emerge through distraction."

For instance, he starts writing the screenplays for his films in his home office on a yellow notepad. When the film's idea takes shape, he systematically rewrites it on the typewriter, the same typewriter he has been using for several decades.

By focusing on specific works that take up a designated number of hours each day and removing the traditional question we ask ourselves, "what should I do next?", he became capable of extracting significant value from the unlimited time spent on his work. This happens every morning of a workday.

Newport adds a satirical title to this paragraph in his article where he mentioned this story, "Focus on works that bring you high value, not Twitter.

"Others finish their films and they go out, and they have a big opening, and they have the critics saying they're great, and it gives them a certain satisfaction. For me, it's like eating a cookie. I finish a film, and I go, 'Now what?' And I start the next one."
Woody Allen

ART AND DEEP WORK

Humanity and Great Minds with Hani Naqshabandi

"Do not strip them of their humanity; they are ordinary people like us, what distinguishes them are two things: continuous perseverance and a deliberate pace of slowing down in order to achieve results in their work. Our problem is that we often idealize and magnify them, thereby stripping them of their humanness and their mistakes. The recipient of this praise finds that we portray them as if they are supernatural beings, when they aren't necessarily so." These were the words of the renowned journalist and esteemed novelist Hani Naqshabandi when I met him with my friend (Mohammad Hisham Hafez), who organized and proposed the meeting in January 2018 at one of the restaurants in "City Walk" in Dubai.

The session was spent in fantastic discussions where we lost track of time, and perhaps his gracious reception of a copy of the book "The Art Revolution: How the Artist Works and How Others Work" was what prompted him to discuss the great minds and artists, leading to the idea here and to the aforementioned comment at the beginning. He added, "I am fascinated by the personality of Einstein, and if you closely observe his life, you will find that he wondered incessantly for a long time, what is light? Why hasn't anyone come before and answered this question for us? The slow thinking and perseverance to explore and discover the answer led him to change humanity and come up with the theory of relativity. I am certain that greatness comes with these two behaviours: slowness (or patience) and perseverance."

He added; "I found that most great minds (and the same applies to writers when we're interested in them) are mostly not successful in other aspects of their lives apart from their specialization. You might find them to be below average, and this is natural, because their mission isn't necessarily to succeed in everything or to dazzle others. Rather, all that matters is a serious attempt to excel in their specialization, their interest and their cause alone." He also commented, "... you will find that continuous perseverance and patience are what have forged and enshrined the names of novelists and writers in history, and they are what made someone like Stalin boldly proclaim over the radio to his people during his war with the Nazis 'Defend the land of Tolstoy and Pushkin,' not 'Defend the land of businessmen or your land.' (Perhaps because literature is what deeply touches the human essence within us, and perhaps because its survival is akin to legacies we inherited that we don't wish to leave behind."

Patience and perseverance are what enable us to create change and touch others. They shape us over time and it may also be said that there is nothing quite like them in terms of influence.

I elaborated extensively in my book "The Art Revolution: How the Artist Works and How Others Work" on the fundamental differences between the life of an artist and the life of a performer or an ordinary employee. Perhaps this isn't the place to recap the most important points covered there. However, I would like to take advantage of this chapter to explore the concept of "deep work" in our lives alongside the notion of "performing work with art".

When we mention Woody Allen, Carl Jung, Einstein, Leo Tolstoy, Michael Jackson, Abdulrahman Al-Sumait, Naguib Mahfouz, Taha Hussein and others, the works they accomplished in their lives come to mind, works that have persisted and continued up until the writing of these lines, without a real insight into the details of their daily lives, day by day.

In deep work, "real work", we see the results and don't see the work being done... and in the "illusion of achievement", we see the work being done and don't see the results.

Perhaps the discerning reader has now greatly understood the significant difference between the illusion of achievement and true work. However, I'd like to approach this topic from another slightly deeper angle. Let's start with a question:

Do you recall the last time in your life when you invested a significant amount of time and effort into a task, project or studying a subject? What was the outcome of that project?... And if it wasn't as positive as you had tried or hoped for, how did you feel after completing the task?

One of the well-known writers, with a subtle touch, mentioned that every time he revisits his old articles and writings that brought him fame, he experiences a type of shock, realizing that he was the one who wrote those articles and humorously would say, "how proud I feel that I am the one who wrote these articles... for a moment, I thought someone else had written them due to their brilliance." I'd like briefly to divert attention from the narcissism of this expression and indeed note that this comment deserves attention. Why did this person find it surprising that he was the one who wrote those articles, as if another person had authored them?

Our Other Version of Deep Work

In reality, that person found it surprising because in actuality it was not the "usual him" who wrote those articles. If you can now connect and answer my question to you: How did you feel after completing the last significant project, you worked on? You will understand what I mean.

Our familiar state is the one that unconsciously responds every day to life's events and interactions. For instance, I don't need to concentrate and have full awareness to drive my car to work daily, and I don't need peak concentration when preparing breakfast or making coffee. This also applies to scrolling through social media channels and most of our traditional daily tasks at work. Even reviewing photos and posts on social media, we find that they are mostly limited moments of concentration that can't be sustained with full awareness and focus. And we do all of this unconsciously.

The known version of us is the one that lives every day with half a mind (if the description fits), and other examples of this include:

- Our response to friends' calls and invitations to go out
- Our immediate response to all WhatsApp messages
- Our choices in food and drink, or settling for the options available in front of us
- Our responses to others' requests without focusing on our ability (or desire) to carry them out
- Our instant acceptance of future social invitations

without reviewing our commitments
- Watching television
- Managing customer affairs or robotically completing tasks scheduled by our managers
- Getting dressed, shaving, showering, picking a place to sit in the living room

These mentioned points are the known version or the natural mode that the general public lives in. If we pause for a moment and compare it to other activities that require a little more depth, we will find a different outcome and a different behaviour.

In other words, when that charming writer embarked on writing one of his remarkable articles (for himself and maybe for others as well), he was at the peak of concentration and mental activity, seriously attempting to formulate a specific idea to put on paper. Simply put, he was a different person, not the ordinary human who responds to his everyday life demands at every moment.

I call this state of consciousness "the art of creation". When that writer revisited what he had previously written, he revisited what his version as an "artist" had produced, not his version as an ordinary human in an ordinary life. This is what led to his surprise, as if someone other than him had done it.

And when you, readers, review your experience in accomplishing a previous work that you were proud of, you have glimpsed over your version as a human (or artist) when you were at the peak of concentration and extraordinary effort in those moments. You are not what you are in a semi-permanent or daily capacity. Just like comparing your usual sitting and performing everyday tasks with engaging in sports, the difference is that the impact of sports will appear on you later and remain with you as long as there is consistency, and perhaps you will feel proud of the result.

An Ordinary Story

I will narrate the following story, assuming it happened to me on one of my days:

1. I woke up in the morning, had breakfast, dropped off my daughter at school, and went to work. I greeted my immediate supervisor and sat at my desk to review emails. Then, I started working on pending tasks related to my clients until noon.

Afterwards, I went out for lunch with a friend with whom I usually have lunch every day. The lunch session wasn't as relaxing and enjoyable as I had expected. Then, I returned to the office, completed the remaining tasks, and dealt with some requests from my direct supervisor. I organized my desk.

After that, I set aside some time to review ticket and hotel prices on the Booking.com website because I was planning a vacation. I received a call from my father, then hung up to call my wife and sister. I quickly asked about their well-being and then I made a final call to a friend, promising to inquire about something he wanted to buy, which my brother owned.

I looked at the clock and saw it was close to five, which meant it was time to head home. I bid farewell to my colleagues and my supervisor, left the office, and went on a short trip to buy a mobile phone cover. Then, I made a quick trip to the supermarket to buy some essentials. I returned home to spend time with my family until nine. After that,

I went out to meet my friends at a cafe and sat with them until eleven at night. Then, I returned home and was in bed by midnight. This routine repeats every day with some variations on weekends.

Now my question: Is there anything strange in this story? And if I told it to you verbally while sitting in front of you, would you find anything strange or interesting in it? Will the story make you laugh, cry, get angry, think or worry? Most likely not.

Because even if it included some detailed additions, such as a problem with someone, a malfunctioning kitchen refrigerator, or a power outage, these wouldn't be significant enough to make you stop and pay attention. They are likely commonplace events that happen frequently under various circumstances and environments, depending on different people and their ages.

2. What if I told you that on that day, before going to lunch, I received a call from a woman I was romantically involved with ten years ago? Her call was like a thunderbolt for me. In a hurried call that didn't exceed ten minutes, she told me that she was struggling with her current husband and wanted to talk to me in an extended conversation to tell me about her circumstances that led her to desire a divorce. She also mentioned that even after all these years, she doesn't trust anyone like the way she blindly trusts me.

What if I told you... that she said to me, "I still love you, I love only you." How am I supposed to deal with this complication? And what if I told you that I could dedicate the next fifty pages to narrate precisely what happened to her in the past, the problems and the societal reasons that led us to part ways, and the whirlwind of emotions I experienced over the years until my marriage? Would you be interested in listening to the story?

I believe that this might stir some interest.

It would be even more captivating if I wrote the story with its detailed circumstances and the genuine feelings that I and the woman experienced. If I attempted to write every moment that caught my attention in my life with her, along with the problems with my family and the sacrifices associated with them, and whatever else I deemed worthy of being written about.

3. What I've mentioned is a story of pure imagination, of course. But the difference between the first and second stories is that I tried to briefly touch on the details of a single phone call that happened during a typical day. Even if I narrated the story in a novel or a short story, someone might notice it and be affected by its events, living their fantasies and stepping out of the realm of reality into the world of narratives and tales. Perhaps someone would respond to me after reading the story, with tears in their eyes, recalling what happened to them while reading, or maybe their eyes teared up just because of the story, no more.

You see, bringing forth a work, art or a story that resonates with others in their lives and manages to change something within them doesn't come about without effort, focus, awareness and intention. It's not merely passing over it as an ephemeral event during the day.

Deep work is when you attempt to shape a story, even if it's confined to a detail that doesn't exceed ten minutes. It can have a far more profound impact than telling the story superficially or in passing (superficial work). And on the surface, if I met my friends and told them the first story, one of them would likely shush me. But perhaps everyone would listen and interact with me if I told them the phone call story with more details and greater depth. The effect would be even stronger if, alongside the story, I conveyed the feelings that haunted me during and after the call.

These two stories are analogous to "the illusion of accomplishment" in the context of the story and "real work." The second story comes with a higher level of description, scrutiny of emotions, memories and situations.

The artistic human

In the realm of articles, stories and various other aspects, deep work (and artistic works or works with an artistic mindset) generally focuses on harnessing the maximum mental or physical capabilities that a person possesses. On the other hand, the illusion of accomplishment centers around repetitive obvious tasks that an individual believes have a tangible impact on others and themselves.

When I dedicate substantial time, effort and intense focus to write a novel, direct a film or create a challenging painting, I immerse myself in its details. Through this process, I might produce a piece that resonates with someone else, and this doesn't happen through mundane tasks that most of us spend our time on.

Flooding social media with advice and catchy words certainly isn't deep work; it might have a slight effect on the recipients. However, sitting down, thinking and working on solving a friend's problem, for instance, constitutes deep work. It's genuine work, not an illusion of accomplishment.

Most enduring and impactful works that have influenced humanity and changed many lives have been created by individuals just like us, with the same physical specifications and the same 24-hour day at their disposal. The only substantial difference is that they invested significant effort, time and study, transforming their work into something remarkable.

I believe that the fundamental difference between the artistic human and the ordinary human is the divergence in focus, time allocation, effort and attention when performing tasks. It's not much else. This awareness initially requires understanding that there are fundamentally two distinct concepts I'm trying (awkwardly) to reiterate through this book: deep work and the illusion of accomplishment.

This applies to nearly everything in our lives. Starting from sending religious messages incessantly on WhatsApp, one could replace this with genuinely influencing others in an attempt to help them. Here, it's worth noting that the concept of deep work also applies to our social relationships. Let's take our relationships with our children as an example. We often hear the Western advice to "spend high-quality time" with your children instead of merely being in their physical presence. Quality time involved things like playing, going out with them and talking to them without being absorbed in your mobile phone. It's probably accurate to say that staying with our children while holding onto our phones and scrolling through social media is just an "illusion of accomplishment," which won't contribute positively to strengthening our relationship with them.

Working with creativity

Personally, I believe that what makes the great figures truly great is their continuous dedication to deep and substantial work, rather than investing more time in less important matters.

Proficient writers understand that the greatest challenge to success as a writer lies in two inseparable aspects: reading extensively and writing extensively. There's no shortcut around this, as the renowned writer Stephen King puts it. Both of these aspects require an element of diligence and discipline. In fact, the quote by author Dorothy Parker holds significant truth, particularly when it comes to understanding writing: "Writing is the art of applying the ass to the seat." This indicates that success in this endeavor doesn't necessarily demand elaborate ideas and extraordinary imagination but rather relies on discipline in actual work by merely sitting down and doing it. The task of discipline becomes more challenging as distractions that distance us from it increase and, as mentioned earlier, there's plenty of those distractions.

Achievement is an Accumulative Process

"Success is an accumulative process…
The well-known author Abdo Khal told me this sentence as he tried to convey his annoyance at some lazy young people who seek quick gains and high positions in their professional lives. He added, "I have been writing since I was seventeen years old but what others now see before them is perhaps a recognized writer. Yet, they forget the years of hard work that have been dedicated to writing over the past thirty years. Success doesn't come overnight."

A READING BETWEEN CREATIVITY AND REPETITION

What is creative work?

I define creative work as work that produces something that has not been done before (or) has not been shared before.

Reaching the level of producing creative work (especially successful work) requires endless hours of deep and slow work, day after day, while understanding flaws of this process and being cautious not to repeat these flaws and at the same time acknowledging that the difficulty of achieving perfection is part of the equation.

This is the opposite of what the collective mind requests and we need more of it.

Creative Work vs. Repetition or Memorization

The problem with repetition is that it's easy, while creative creation is difficult.

The behaviours and prevalent beliefs of others often encourage repetition of most interactions in various aspects of our lives. These interactions don't demand much thought or creativity. I find that society and schools, for example, encourage memorization (even in the 21st century) despite technology making information readily available.

This prevailing attitude is why you often see respectable families motivating their children to memorize without adequately promoting the skills of contemplation, reflection and creativity. This is not a declaration of my opposition to memorization but rather a call to reconsider the mechanism of promoting deep study, contemplation and creative work alongside memorization, to balance them.

Most books in humanity's history were not written with the purpose of memorization as opposed to utilization, application and benefit. The comparison is also pertinent in that reading and repeating what is in this book before me won't benefit the reader if done mechanically or just parroted to others. I might not display any signs of awe if someone told me they've memorized this book cover to cover, without comprehension, thought or discussion of its contents.

Creativity is forged through deep thought and profound

connections between pre-existing ideas and content, allowing the creators to synthesize new compositions, works or innovative ideas that enrich their lives.

Why Don't Our Minds Work as We Want Them To?

Why is it difficult for the mind to capture a new idea in a state of conscious awareness and deliberate thought, while it captures easily when the subconscious mind is dozing or unaware? Dr. Ali AlWardi wonders. It seems that the conscious mind has an analytical rather than a compositional nature. It can research, think and investigate but it can create very little. Perhaps the secret lies in the fact that the conscious mind tends to focus and be precise in observation. When studying something, it attempts to concentrate on a single point. Consequently, it's not easy for it to grasp multiple points with a single glance. During research, it gathers ideas and delves into their details, yet it cannot connect two distant ideas. AlWardi adds in another context, somewhat sarcastically, regarding memorization enthusiasts:

"This is the reason we see among the memorizers those who are unable to comprehend or innovate. They are adept at memorizing information, repeating it and parroting it. However, they remain like parrots, incapable of extracting any benefit from what they've memorized. On the contrary, the inspired geniuses work to understand diverse ideas and then forget them. The meaning is that they leave these ideas stored in the depths of their subconscious minds, where they interact and interconnect. Hence, they excel in responding and are more capable of problem-solving than those excessive in memorization."

In this simplified analysis, AlWardi might address three important issues that we also encounter in our daily lives:

We should not fear forgetting what we read because the content will be stored in our subconscious minds and will resurface as creative ideas or solutions to problems we face in our lives. Here lies the essence of "creativity". Furthermore, AlWardi comments in another place (and I very much agree with this remark), "Creators cannot create something out of nothing; they compose from pre-existing things. Their virtue lies only in the act of connecting and assembling."

Don't worry about yourself or your children if they struggle with memorization in school subjects. Most likely, you'll find your child memorizing names and dates of beloved figures instinctively because they perceive these as worthy of memorization. In this time, what's worth memorizing, you'll surely find, is worth searching for anytime on Google.

We must realize that the topics of memorization and creativity are matters of choice, not an inherent capacity. If you value memorization, then you should work on it. It's not necessary that you match the efficiency of analysis and utilization with your capacity for memorization. The more importance you attach to memorization, the more your inclination towards contemplation, questioning and understanding might unconsciously diminish.

Where is the Link between creativity and deep work?

The concise answer is: in the attempt to create something or influence others.

Creating value, generating solutions or producing works that endure over extended periods in our lives – creativity involves this. Creativity isn't profound if it doesn't persist for a significant period of time, achieving results beyond our limited spheres in this world. With a bit of observation, we note a contrast between the everyday realism of an individual engaged in deep work and the results that emerge from their creative efforts, which transcend our preconceptions.

Sometimes, the unassuming appearance of a person engrossed in deep work, or their attire and demeanour, can be captivating. It's as if appearances suggest that monumental creations are associated with physically or mentally exceptional individuals, even though they might not surpass ordinary individuals in their physical or intellectual capabilities outside their realm of creativity. Here, we spontaneously wonder when we encounter a creative person: "Is this the person who drew or wrote that thing, or directed or established that billion-dollar company?"

Nevertheless, we forget that what this creative individual has accomplished might actually involve this person being used to not appearing in our view – there is no visible achievement – due to being occupied by work and a rigorous, disciplined schedule. They might not be overly concerned with, or influenced by, what affects the general public. The masses find it easier to replicate what others like them are doing, without delving deeply into matters that demand considerable effort and persistence. Creative creation and the persistence in deep work can be challenging for them. They may perceive that creative or successful individuals are intrinsically linked to the concepts of genius or luck, without focusing much on the effort and time invested.

The pursuit of easy solutions, combined with the lack of emphasis on discipline and deep work in our lives, leads to questioning creative individuals in ways that might not directly contribute to our success.

After renowned author and novelist Stephen King finishes his official encounters with the audience, he concludes the sessions with a traditional question to them: "Any questions?" On one occasion, an attendee asked, "Stephen, what type of pencils do you use for writing?" – as if the type of pencil used would transform the inquirer into a good writer.

PART 4: IMPLEMENTATION

THE EQUATION OF EFFORT VERSUS TIME

"We exert very little effort to challenge our minds to evolve in various domains," says the psychologist and researcher on human expertise and competencies Anders Ericsson, and he adds, "It is unfortunate that we often accept that because we become content when we say to ourselves that what we do is 'good enough'. And in truth, what we do is indeed good enough. However, it's important to be aware that there is another option available, which is that if we want to become better at anything we practice; we simply can do it better."

In his book "Peak: Secrets from the New Science of Expertise", Ericsson focuses on the concept of human performance development through what he calls "deliberate practice". He succinctly defines it as follows:

"Deliberate practice is practicing a specific type of activity for the purpose of achieving a long-term goal through systematic and regular training. While regular practice may involve meaningless repetition, deliberate practice requires focused attention and is carried out to achieve a specific goal, which is improving performance in the activity we are training for."

From this, we understand that repeating (or imitating) any action, exercise or practice without a methodical and clear approach does not lead us to progress to a more advanced stage; instead, it might even be a waste of time.

For example, walking four kilometres a day might be challenging in the beginning but over time the body adapts to it and the desired effect of walking this distance diminishes. Nonetheless, walking with less impact is still better than not walking at all. However, we must recognize that under the concept of "deliberate practice" the effect of this walking exercise differs and its condition changes, if we aim to develop our performance or even consider such an idea. If walking four kilometres takes us forty minutes and we repeat this walk regularly, it becomes a normal repetitive exercise. But if we set a goal, such as completing the same four kilometres in less time or striving to walk longer distances, and then progress to transforming walking into jogging or running, and then further push to run longer distances in less time on a regular basis, this progression falls under the category of "deliberate practice" rather than mere repetition.

Ericsson's book is not about developing one's task performance or physical exercise or any skill-related training. I will convey my observations to readers in the moments to come.

Ericsson also comments on people's perceptions towards the concept of exercise and the extraordinary abilities they see in others. He says:

"People generally believe that the performance of experts (or most successful individuals in their fields) differs qualitatively from ordinary performance, as they think that experts should possess qualitatively distinct characteristics from those possessed by novices. We partially agree with this. However, we deny that these differences are immutable. In this context, it may be appropriate to address the topic of innate talents from another perspective, namely, that there are indeed exceptional cases among very few individuals who possess innate talents that we believe are unique to them that cannot be acquired by others. The most prominent exceptions are those who possess genetic traits. Nevertheless, we assert that the (radical) differences between successful performers and those who master their work (or arts) compared to others stem primarily from the fact that successful performers usually engage in deliberate practice in what they do, rather than possessing extraordinary abilities."

My comment: In reality, anyone, like me, who practices the profession of writing, can discover the extent of slowness and lack of focus that affects them after they stop writing for a period of time, and vice versa. When we know that many other writers in this world can produce over two thousand words a day, for example, we may as writers feel frustrated and forget that achieving a consistent output of over two thousand words daily requires deliberate practice. I humbly emphasize this point as related to the writing profession.

I believe that discussing this concept or the idea of deliberate practice might be worth including in our discussions with athletes around us, for instance, as well as artists, composers, musicians, chess players and even with the restaurant or hotel worker in the "buffet" section who rapidly shapes the "Mutabbaq"[9] dough in an impressive and skilful way. Let's explore and discover that this concept is

---

9 "Mutabbaq" is a popular dish in Saudi Arabia. It is a square-shaped, fried or baked, thin layer of bread stuffed mainly with minced meat, eggs, leeks, green onion and cut in further smaller squares after cooking, it is served with lemon and green chilli.

true to a great extent and that deliberate practice has indeed led them to a high level of focus, skill and mastery.

Deliberate practice requires a lot of time, discipline, focus and awareness of its significance before embarking on it, in order for us to move from one level to another, higher level. Continuously attempting to reach a new level through deliberate practice is a form of deep work.

It's worth mentioning that one of the major opponents of deliberate practice is the behaviour of "illusion of accomplishment," which we feel when we show or share with others a small amount of practice in something (or even repeat it without improvement) to achieve an instant sense of satisfaction. Every day, when we post an image that gives us the illusion of accomplishment on social media channels, we get preoccupied with it due to the sense of accomplishment, unfortunately neglecting the need for real and continuous effort.

The more we focus on the importance of immediate satisfaction, the less we pay attention to the necessity of continuous improvement, subconsciously, in what we do.

I strongly support the idea for all of us to reduce the amount of sharing what we do with others and to compensate it by focusing more on the work itself.

Where does the illusion of achievement fit here?

I hope that the idea I'm trying to convey, that through focusing on effort versus time in continuous practice to develop a specific skill or task, can be considered as the antipathy to the behaviour of shallow repetition, which we know for sure is an illusion of accomplishment.

Going back to the author Cal Newport... he finds that the ability of most of us to send a number of emails and attend meetings during the day requires very basic skills that do not necessitate a large amount of creativity, expertise or exceptional abilities. When one spends most of the working day drowned by responding to emails, attending meetings and providing routine replies to customer requests while solving some problems, they become a repetitive copy of most employees.

In fact, this may lead their immediate supervisor to consider replacing them with another employee who performs these tasks, in order to get a new employee who is cheaper or a little faster. Think about it! If you were in their supervisor's position and had the opportunity to hire a new employee instead of the old one, with a lower salary and a slightly faster pace, would you consider it?

Due to the ease of repeating some tasks, the majority settle for what Ericsson calls the "good enough" mindset in their lives, and they don't try to step out of their comfort zone to challenge themselves to develop a specific skill or ability to elevate it.

Seeing the salary deposited into the account every month, along with relatively straightforward tasks, unfortunately triggers a mental complacency in most of us. We don't feel the need for any challenges or exceptions. Just like the kind-hearted brother who continuously sends massive preaching messages to others in pursuit of receiving his own reward without spending much time and effort on real, actual work that produces benefits and rewards at the same time.

Identifying where time and effort are spent

When we find a successful person around us who is disciplined and outstanding in his career, we subconsciously think of one of the following negative judgments about the person:
1. Because this person is not available to others most of the time, we might find within our minds that he is an arrogant person or we may even see him as socially deficient. We ignore that his discipline is a natural state and a direct reason for his success.
2. We create a thousand excuses for ourselves that this person is creative and has innate talents that we can't necessarily possess like him. We forget that this person is successful and skilled in his work because he is disciplined, not the other way around.

And our conventional problem in society is that we don't consciously pay as much attention to beginnings, routines and discipline as we do to being amazed by the result, which can be quite obvious. Everyone knows that humans have limitations they can't exceed, such as degree of physical energy, how many hours in a day they can usefully function and the limitations of mental abilities. What actually happens in reality is that as humans, we redistribute these capacities to different matters. This distribution is what defines who we are, what we do and what we've achieved, or as someone put it in a meaningful description: "A person is a product of their solitude."

The intelligent person is the one who spends more time and effort than their less intelligent counterpart in endeavors that have made them smarter, even if they're not consciously aware of it. In all truth, a fair comparison of two young people of the same age, in terms of the results they've achieved, is impossible if one of them spent the past five years reading books and doing research, alongside some other efforts, while the other spent the same time watching TV, playing card game, and smoking shisha.

Minimization, Not Addition

The first rule in attempting to develop, accomplish and create real work in any practice we engage in within our lives, especially amid the clutter of information and the illusion of achievements, is "minimizing" what we believe to be an accomplishment, which is, in fact, is an illusion of accomplishment.

Reducing four scattered hours during the day spent on social media platforms is the first step to begin writing our new book or creating our next piece of artwork. Subtracting an hour out of the two hours spent in the evening watching TV is the start towards more achievement by reading additional books.

It doesn't require much theorizing to tell readers that closing the windows of superficial tasks and the bad habits we engage in every day is the basis for building better new habits. Time is limited and it's established; it's either spent on real work or on the illusion of accomplishment.

Those two hours in the evening could be spent at the coffee shop socializing, every day, for example, or they could be utilized to build our new project. It's an either-or situation; the two do not exist side by side.

Indeed, the idea of reducing the time spent on the illusion of accomplishment, such as our companionship and spending time with friends whom we know truly do not add any value to our lives, is considered the first step towards surrounding ourselves with friends of greater intellectual and moral value. The concept of reduction applies in one direction, automatically replacing it in another direction.

Being aware that we deceive ourselves into thinking we've achieved something is step "zero", and step "one" is to rid ourselves of this.

In this regard, writer and researcher Eric Barker, author of the book "Barking Up the Wrong Tree", provides some interesting insights. He maintains that much of what we previously knew about success is often based on misconceptions. He says, "Why do we insist on engaging in matters that hold no value in our lives? Perhaps we tell ourselves it's because we're lazy or weak, and that might be somewhat true, but more often than not, it's not precisely the case. This is because we can become what we want to be in terms of success, while simultaneously embracing the idea that by quitting things that don't add value to our lives or directly contribute to our aspirations, we become much less stressed and less tense. And when we ask who are the people experiencing stress in their lives specifically due to this, we discover that they are the people who haven't quit things that don't provide any value or benefit in their lives. Perseverance isn't achieved without quitting things that don't add any value to us."

We humans are always seeking more: more health, more pleasure, more energy. But in our real lives, the assumed answer is actually the exact opposite. In reality, we need to reduce and minimize.

We need less stress in our lives, fewer distractions and fewer responsibilities. Do we need more time spent watching TV (or any distracting pastime)? No. Rather, we need as little of it as possible, in order to focus on specific goals in

MINIMIZATION, NOT ADDITION

which we want to succeed.

And the question here is, what will you reduce in your life in order to engage in more important matters instead? Imagine that you have poor health and can accomplish only one task daily. What would that be? Congratulations, now you've identified the crucial task in your life that you want to pursue. This is what should consume more of your hours and it's what you need to accomplish before anything else. You'll know where to allocate your perseverance efforts and where to quit other matters, or as the old saying goes, "You can accomplish anything, you just can't accomplish everything". You might even ask yourself: If I quit everything unimportant, will I become too frugal to interact with most aspects of my life? Actually, this is precisely the opinion of the young writer Ryan Holiday on this matter: "To create your own real work, you'll be forced to ask yourself: What am I willing to sacrifice in order to achieve this work? Should I sacrifice this and that?"

Being prepared to sacrifice (or reduce) in terms of spare time, comfort, easily earned money and status always lies at the heart of achieving great works, sometimes significantly and sometimes less so. But there's always a crucial sacrifice involved in something. And if not, all humans would find it easy to accomplish great works.

The same concept is approached from a different angle by writer and researcher Jim Collins. In his book "Good to Great: Why Some Companies Make the Leap and Others Don't", he emphasizes that the tasks of successful CEOs when managing their companies often begin with discontinuing inferior or valueless products and removing them from the market before attempting to introduce new products or strategies to attract new customers.

Steve Jobs and minimalism

The initial tasks that were assigned to Steve Jobs when he took over the management of Apple in 1997 focused on getting rid of most of the existing products within the company. The aim was to concentrate efforts and time on the most important products. This concept is explained by Walter Isaacson in his book "Steve Jobs", where he states, "A review of the products revealed the lack of focus that Apple had. The company was producing multiple versions of each product due to bureaucracy and catering to the desires of retail stores." He further adds, "Apple had multiple versions of the Macintosh computer, each with a different number causing confusion, and these numbers ranged from 1400 to 9600."

Steve Jobs himself spoke about this: "I had the employees explain each product to me over three weeks. But in the end, I understood nothing." He concluded this explanation by asking his team, "Which of these products should I recommend to my friends to buy?"

When he couldn't get simple answers, Steve Jobs was swift in deciding to eliminate these models and products with seventy percent of them being discarded. He told one group responsible for product design, "You are bright people, don't waste your time on these poor products."

Steve Jobs claimed that good engineers, including those whose products were cancelled, were grateful for his actions.

At an Apple employee meeting in September 1997, Jobs said, "I left the meeting with people whose products were cancelled but they were at the peak of happiness after leaving a meeting because they finally understood where they were headed."

We can extrapolate the idea I'm trying to convey about comprehending real work in the context of the individual when we compare "retail stores" to "others" or the general public. We sincerely believe that owning more things will contribute to a better image of ourselves and that when we show others our superficial actions that don't carry real value, this gives us the illusion that we are great people (with the illusion of accomplishment). While this may be relatively true, it's a temporary state where we can't focus on creating value or even impressing others with what we do.

Additionally, it's worth reminding readers of a famous figure who works in various fields such as fashion and management studies, and is also an inspiration to others and intends to write a book. Entrepreneurs or those seeking excellent marketing tools for their products may hire her, not for any of these specialties, but for her looks and the number of followers she has.

In this context, I remember a newly opened restaurant that claimed to specialize in the Indian cuisine. Due to my long term enthusiasm for Indian food, I didn't hesitate to visit the restaurant. However, after examining the menu during my visit, I discovered that they took pride in offering Chinese and Asian dishes in general, along with pizza options, in addition to Indian food. The menu was highly diversified and detailed, unfortunately leading me to leave without attempting to explore what this place intended to offer.

Returning to the subject matter regarding Apple, the first

step to elevate the company to a new level was reduction, followed by clarity of focus and perseverance as clearly seen by the cancellation of seventy percent of the products Apple used to sell in the market. If the field is always left open (to others), they would have demanded more of everything without awareness. If we think a little about this matter, we'll find it greatly applies to our ordinary lives as individuals. Most likely, close friends and family might appreciate you owning more of everything and being into everything, while ignoring that as an ambitious person seeking to build a better life, you should focus on reducing matters to devote yourself to the most important things in your life. Through this reduction, over time, you will realize that what you were occupied with was in your best interest and the interest of others.

The Things That Don't Change

Jeff Bezos, the CEO of Amazon, always tells his employees, "Focus on the things that don't change." This principle was translated into action when he focused on the most crucial element in his company, something that remains unchanged no matter how many years pass: the speed and cost-effectiveness of shipping products sold to the company's customers. Advertising even stopped completely and budgets were redirected towards developing shipping infrastructure, eventually leading to free shipping for Amazon Prime subscribers and later settling into the policy of free shipping for all orders exceeding twenty-five dollars.

I find that the emphasis on things that should not change in our lives from our perspective to be one of the projections we need to pay attention to. There are indeed things that should not change, in contrast to the "reduction" of things that should change.

The question we should ask ourselves here is: What are the things that should not change in our lives? A summary of this philosophy would proclaim: Possessing more things is not a measurement of happiness and is certainly not the most critical measure of success. The difference between a successful person and an extremely successful person is often that the latter frequently says "no", as the well-known businessman Warren Buffett had disclosed.

PRODUCTIVITY AND DEEP WORK

The To-Do List and the Difference Between an Option and a Choice

We, as enthusiastic young individuals interested in the concepts of productivity and accomplishment, often create "to-do lists" during our workdays. We write down on paper, notebooks or our phones the tasks we intend to complete throughout the day. More often than not, we fill them with more than five tasks. The day usually ends without completing all of them.

The problem with the to-do list, when written, is that it doesn't take into account two important factors while attempting to accomplish it:
1. How much time should be allocated for each task?
2. How much free time do you have, and where will it be allotted during your day?

Without considering these questions, you'll stumble in your efforts, often letting random tasks overshadow what you should actually be doing (or stopping what you shouldn't be doing) at a specific moment in your schedule. The key here is that you won't be able to get things done. "Defining specific tasks and allocating time for their accomplishment (rather than just writing them down) is the solution," as Cal

Newport comments.

So, the idea is simple: allocate specific time slots on your schedule (I recommend using a phone calendar) for when you want to complete specific tasks.

Assigning work tasks to specific time slots will guide you away from thinking about what you should invest your time in; the decision has already been made. Differentiate the time you allocate between urgent smaller tasks and bigger tasks that require more time.

Over time, you will technically become more adept at predicting the actual time you need for your work-related tasks, or for your overall work times.

For instance, if you need to make four phone calls to accomplish specific tasks, ask yourself: How long will each call likely take? Fifteen minutes at most? Then, this approach suggests dedicating an hour in your workday to make those four calls. How long does it take to prepare a presentation for a client? Two hours? Allocate two hours of your schedule for that task during your day.

You might initially feel frustrated because the realistic number of daily hours doesn't match the magnitude of tasks you've assigned to yourself (as we tend to do), and that's okay. This experience will certainly guide you to have a better shot at ensuring productivity, even if it means having fewer tasks that you can actually accomplish. Achieving a little realistically is better than not achieving at all.

Furthermore, this approach can be considered one of the most important ways to drop the idea of increasing rather than reducing. Reduction in favor of something practical is better than expanding tasks that won't be accomplished.

Moreover, this approach can be easily applied to

scheduling leisure activities, family commitments and social engagements in our lives. It can also be used to prioritize and execute tasks as soon as they're scheduled.

For those interested: Here's an example from my calendar for one of my workdays, as an attempt to apply "scheduling".
7:00 AM: Breakfast - Serene's school drop-off
8:30 AM Meditation session
9:00 AM Writing time - Book
1:00 PM Visit to Ministry of Commerce to obtain an extract
2:00 PM Lunch
3:00 PM Review contract and send it via voice message
3:15 PM Write article for my blog
3:45 PM Review contract and follow up with content author
4:00 PM Make four phone calls to follow up with colleagues and book distributors
5:00 PM Task closure + respond to emails + planning for tomorrow
5:45 PM Jogging + dinner + putting daughters to sleep
8:00 PM Reading

Tom Ford

"What does it mean to go out together (or hang out)?" comments the well-known fashion designer Tom Ford in response to his host Jimmy Kimmel's question. He continues, "I don't understand when a friend talks to me and says, 'Let"s go out in the evening'. Where are we going to go and when exactly? I know something called 'Let's have dinner at 7:30,' and I know 'Let's set aside a specific time for going out (from this time to that time).' But I don't understand what it means when someone suddenly says, 'Let's go out, now.'"

Kimmel asks him before that: "You're a screenwriter, director and producer of movies, and in addition to that, you're the designer and the head of a well-known fashion brand that bears your name. I'm very surprised. How do you manage all of that? I really want to know, how do you do it?"

Ford responds with a single word: "Scheduling." He then explains, "I'm very, very organized in my schedule. Some friends scold me when I ask them: 'What does it mean to go out together?' I can handle the idea that says 'Let's allocate time from this hour to that hour' to go out together (and considers anything else as disorganized time wasting)." He adds, "In the fashion industry, many activities repeat every year. That's why I'm not joking when I say I schedule my days for an entire year in advance." So, you don't relax? You work all the time, Kimmel comments. Ford replies,

"On the contrary, there are times for rest. It's true that I think and work all the time, but once you work in the field you're passionate about, what you do doesn't feel like work anymore. It becomes enjoyment."

Don't Break the Chain

For years, software developer Brad Isaac recounted an experience when he was performing his role as a "comedian" at an event. He shared that he received the best advice ever from Jerry Seinfeld when he asked him about the secret to his overwhelming success as a comedian. Considering Seinfeld's prolific output and continued success over two decades, Isaac explained the simple method of his success as follows:

"Every January (or every month), I put up a large calendar page on the wall and on the first day, I write a new comedic text. After completing this task, I draw a big 'X' with a red pen on that day. I derive satisfaction on that day only after drawing that 'X' to tell myself that I've accomplished what I needed to. Do this on the following day, and then the day after that, and afterwards, you'll have only one goal: Don't break the chain."

The importance of having a solid daily routine in the lives of many artists was extensively discussed in the book "The Art Revolution: How the Artist Works and How Others Work." I still believe in this principle today – that one of the most crucial secrets to success and leaving an impact in our lives and the lives of those around us doesn't necessarily stem from anything other than continuous effort.

When one of us commits to accomplishing at least one task for deep work, and insists on allocating time for it every day without fail, marking an 'X' on each day when the accomplishment is achieved, we're genuinely positively shocked by our performance and productivity within a few days.

The 'X' symbolizes discipline and achievement. From another perspective, it signifies that each day we're progressing toward achieving deep work and distancing ourselves from the illusion of accomplishment. Consistent perseverance and a measured pace in execution are what make the difference and impact on us and others, not just striving for attention or excessive use of "social media". Even if 'X' is dedicated to deep work for just one hour per week, it would amount to fifty-two hours of profound effort throughout the year. I hope we don't underestimate the significance of small and continuous achievements.

Even as I write these lines, those around me know that the few hours preceding noon, until 12:00 PM, are off-limits, dedicated to deep work in my life (specifically my writing activities). I'm uncertain whether this may change in the future, but I'm serious about safeguarding this time and this task for deep work nearly every day. I've replaced the 'X' with a block that covers most of the early morning hours in my mobile calendar. And, without pretence, it is my wish to be able to continue this practice for life.

Even if I complete various tasks of "illusion of accomplishment" at other times during the day, I'll assure myself that I'm still doing well and on the right track, as long as the most crucial part of my day is pre-determined for the most important matters in my life.

THE RELATIONSHIP BETWEEN WORDS AND TAKING ACTION

"The relationship between 'talk' and 'work' is that one kills the other"
- **Ryan Holiday**

Actress, comedienne and writer Sarah Silverman has often been asked by aspiring writers, "I want to become a writer, how do I do it?" Instead of giving them generic praise, suggesting they read her works, or telling them it's possible, Silverman responds directly: "Start writing. Writers write. Nobody is going to hire you to write."

Whenever Casey Neistat, one of the most successful filmmakers on YouTube, is presented with movie ideas from someone, he responds with, "I don't want to hear your ideas. The idea is the easy part." He understands that in the realm of creativity, the concept of ideas being cheap is essential. Every individual has some form of an idea. The real challenge lies in execution. "You have to focus on the execution," comments Ryan Holiday, adding, "No one else is going to do the work you want to do."

Working on My Next Novel

In his small book entitled "Working on My Next Novel", satirical writer Cory Arcangel compiles tweets and posts from dozens of individuals who eagerly announce across various social media platforms that they've started writing novels. The writer sarcastically highlights that many of these people tweet about writing but aren't actually writing novels in reality.

Although the book's content may be quite superficial, collecting tweets only from those who claim to be writing and including their names and timestamps, its purpose becomes clear through its documentation and publication. It highlights a common tendency among many of us to seek praise before completing actual work, work that might deserve some praise.

The problem with announcing unfinished work and contracts formed between individuals and entities without tangible results (as mentioned in a previous chapter) is that it often leads to non-accomplishment. The presence of social media has exacerbated this by allowing the announcer of an upcoming project to falsely project an accomplishment they haven't actually achieved, giving them that well-known "instant gratification".

Just stating that I'm going to work on project X or novel Y is enough to garner some positive responses, and many times people stop at this exhilaration without pursuing the actual work. The work that requires hours and days of concentration, which might eventually turn each of us into a true artist.

Comparing ourselves to others

Choosing deep work and dedicating mental effort and time to it usually goes hand in hand with comparing ourselves to others in our surroundings. There's always that person whose level of achievements we aspire to reach but have not yet reached. The significant societal challenge lies in the fact that personal advertisements and excessive self-presentation online hardly differentiate between actual accomplishments in reality and the superficial representation on social media. Additionally, the prevalence of advice culture and continuous preaching in our society can lead recipients to believe that these self-proclaimed experts practice exactly what they preach, when in reality they are ordinary individuals, facing life's challenges, just like us.

"The problem with attention is that it's limited, either given by a failed individual from the forum or given by a successful individual. Unfortunately, the scale tips in favor of the unsuccessful person," says the esteemed Emirati visual artist Mattar bin Lahej. He adds, "Any person with a little effort can present themselves in official gatherings, without anyone questioning whether this person truly deserves the momentum they've gained or whether they will provide real value to others. In fact, I've been surprised on several occasions that the presenters of workshops in our artistic field, for example, often don't even know the basics of the lessons they should be giving. But keep in mind that the recipient doesn't really differentiate in this matter because they are not experts anyway."

For a while now, I've been greatly impressed by some individual achievements (some on a daily basis) of those I follow in Western society.

Ryan Holiday, the young writer and known marketer, runs eleven kilometres daily in fifty minutes, and has been reading the equivalent of two hundred and fifty books a year since 2007. He lives on a farm and writes a book each year, sometimes even two, without neglecting his long articles (most of which exceed a thousand words) that he publishes every week. Of course, he's married, has a child and manages his own company.

Another person I follow on "Goodreads" goes by the name "Hadrian". He managed to read two hundred books in 2017. When that year ended, he expressed mild frustration, almost like an apology, for the relatively low number of books he had read compared to previous years. He justified this by mentioning that he was recently promoted at work, making him busier than before. He also noted that most of the books he read in 2017 were heavy and voluminous (some exceeding one thousand five hundred pages).

Stephen King, who happens to be my personal hero and mentor, completed three heavy works in 2017, the most recent being the novel "Sleeping Beauties" with his son, Owen King, surpassing seven hundred pages. Stephen King is now in his mid-seventies and his productivity, abundance and discipline are even more remarkable than they were in his youth. This is besides his involvement in producing numerous successful films and series on Netflix in recent years, which you'd notice if you're a subscriber.

If I were to provide the readers with more examples (there are dozens), I fear you might become a bit discouraged. I often reiterate that our problem during upbringing... upbringing that might not have shaped us to be as persevering in various aspects of life as we could have been. Two things truly stand out to me about the individuals mentioned: firstly, their lifestyle includes exponentially more distractions and entertainment options than we have, yet it hasn't affected them. Secondly, they were already successful. If, hypothetically, one of them stops (they've accomplished a lot already), their previous successes would still vouch for their real work rate.

Comparing oneself and aspiring to emulate someone in our narrow circle may not necessarily be an enticing choice, at least for me. Comparing oneself to the aspirations and achievements of others anywhere on Earth pushes you to focus on achieving a part of what they've accomplished, distancing you from many of the illusory accomplishments in your surroundings. Regrettably, this might require substantial effort while searching for true heroes.

DEEP WORK AND EXTENDED TIME

Competence isn't achieved overnight. Entrepreneur Warren Buffett points out that what you're trying to achieve from your list of twenty-five goals may take you years to accomplish. That's why Buffett encourages others to focus on the five most important goals and completely disregard the rest.

Reducing goals and focusing on the top five while minimizing distractions might exponentially surprise us with exceptional achievements year after year.

Amr Diab

One question put to Amr Diab on the Rotana Channel was: "Are you always, always like this… so focused on your work?" This was just before his performance in 2009. This comment was a gentle way of addressing his near-complete absence from interviews and media appearances.

Those with a superficial knowledge of Amr Diab will know that this singer can almost make people not realize he has a voice outside of singing. I would assume that his interview with Rotana before entering the concert in that year was done under certain pressure or a specific agreement that somewhat embarrassed him, as he sat uncomfortably with the host and repeated more than once: "Ok! Ok! I'm coming to you now.. when I'm done!"

Amr Diab has been singing since 1982, and I wouldn't want to waste the readers' time by listing his accomplishments and record-breaking numbers. What is known about him - outside of his musical endeavours - are two things: his limited engagement with the media regarding his private life, and his attractive youthful appearance that makes him look much younger than his age. The latter attribute would not have come without the former, in my opinion.

We've almost never heard of any major issues or dramas with Amr Diab in the past thirty years. His fans were continuously receiving a stream of his works without getting caught up in issues that they weren't supposed to be concerned with. I find myself today, for example, as one of his fans who doesn't want and shouldn't be obligated to watch his movements, personal problems and sensitive situations he's encountered in his life. I presume I'm quite busy with a family and responsibilities of my own, which naturally won't prevent me from enjoying his songs.

Recently, I followed his Instagram account, only to discover that most of his posts depict him working out at the gym. If I were to view this positively, not neutrally, I would say that a person born in 1961, who enjoys a significant fan base, deserves to share his daily trips to the gym with others. Maybe, just maybe, this personal endeavor could motivate me. Amr Diab has maintained most of his team members for over fifteen years, as well as his family (including his wife) without change. The same spirit, fitness and momentum remain unchanged as well.

In my personal analysis of his accomplishments and works, I found that many simple and difficult factors had come together behind his success. He's consistently receptive to new works and it's unlikely they'd accept works from him that contradict his established history. If I were to sum it all up in one word, it would be "consistency".

Notice that his work has hardly ever ceased since the beginning of his artistic journey. There's no way he could have stayed at the same level if he were occupied with ordinary matters of life (like social media addiction or talking more than working). He's found a balance to continue his work while still being involved in life and he's even found room for personal matters, like his physical health, fitness and family.

I personally believe Amr Diab has divided his life into the following categories (in no particular order):

1. Family (or his personal circle)
2. His studio (and everything related to his work and productions)
3. Healthy eating and exercise (his general health and well-being).

As for matters of lesser importance in his life, they probably include anything else that is not mentioned in the previous points.

Someone might ask: Are all of Amr Diab's songs amazing? Of course not.

But the sheer volume of his production has overshadowed the flaws in songs that didn't resonate with everyone, or as renowned writer Ray Bradbury puts it: "Quantity produces quality."

Any artist in any field cannot expect to receive prestigious awards for their first work — save in very rare cases. Universal law demonstrates the connection of perseverance to success and the human way doesn't accept every work an artist directly produces. The yearning for extraordinary achievements is often followed by a plethora of failures.

I find that the incessant appearances of social media celebrities without continuous deep and focused work on projects deserving of time and effort have created a dilemma in the formula of success. They probably think that their constant visibility without substantial value or work will earn them more attention and take more space from others who truly deserve it.

The problem with media these days is that it portrays us all the time, and what I fear from continuous appearances on social media without real value or work are two things: First, trivial content (regardless of the field) is spreading rapidly and taking much of our focus and attention throughout the day. When you ask yourself at the end of the day: What did you learn? Or what did you gain? I'll answer and say that spending more time reading a book would have definitely been better for you. Second, good content doesn't occupy that same space quickly; it requires ongoing effort from its creator to work on it and produce it, in order to steal a larger share from the inferior works. But my only consolation is that the latter aspect is what truly makes a difference in the lives of the recipients, and it's the one that lasts longer.

From my limited exploration of Amr Diab's life, I have learned the following important lessons:

1. Focus on work and spare your audience from insignificant matters
2. Consistency in work, every day and every year, without exception
3. Accepting continuous failures in some of your work to eventually produce something truly worthwhile
4. Creating small circles of priorities and letting go of less important matters

In 1982, he moved to Cairo and joined the Higher Institute of Arabic Music. In 1983, Amr recorded his first song, "Al Zaman" (Lyrics: Hani Zaki, Music: Hany Shenouda), and released his first album "Ya Tareeq" in the same year. In 1984, he recorded his second album "Ghanny Men Albak". In 1985, he released his third album "Ya Helwa".

In 1986, Amr graduated from the institute, and his album "Hala Hala" was released. In the same year, he made his first appearance in cinema alongside Ilham Shahin and Youssef Shaaban in the movie "Al Sijnatayn".

In 1987, he released the album "Khallast Ghair Rasmi",

which was preceded by an unofficial album entitled "Asif La Yoojad Hal Akher" in the same year.

In 1988, his album "Mayyal" marked the beginning of his collaboration with artist Hamid El Shaeri in music distribution. In 1989, he released the album "Shawqana", and in the same year, he appeared in the film "Al Afareet" alongside Madiha Kamel.

In 1990, Amr was chosen to represent Egypt in the fifth African Nations Cup, where he sang in English and French. The TV concert was broadcast via satellite in the Arab world and featured on CNN. He then released the album "Ma Takhafysh", and its music video was shown in North America, making Amr the first young Arab singer to be featured on a Canadian TV channel in Washington.

In 1991, he released the album "Habibi," which featured the use of saxophone for the first time in his work. In the same year, he starred in the film "Ice Cream in Gleem", alongside a cast of stars, and released an album featuring songs from the movie.

In 1993, he released the album "Ya Omrena", which confirmed his popularity among the masses, especially with the song "Kan 'Andak Haqq". In the same year, he opened the Egyptian Cinema Festival with the film "Amr Dihik Wa La'ab", alongside Omar Sharif and Yousra, in the directorial debut of Tarek Al Telmisani.

In 1994, he released the album "Wi'Lomoni", which showcased the integration of Amr's music with Spanish guitar for the first time. The same year saw the release of the album "Zekrayat", which featured songs from the films "Dihik Wa La'ab" and "Jad Wa Hab".

In 1995, he released the album "Rag'een", which he

presented in concerts in Egypt, Lebanon and Kuwait. In the same year, he performed at Carthage and Syria, achieving widespread success.

In 1996, he released the album "Oudouni", and in the same year, he signed a contract with Rotana after leaving Alam El Phan. He also appeared in concerts in Dubai and Kuwait.

In 1997, he released the album "Awedony", which achieved huge sales from its first days of release. He also won the Africa Music Award.

In 1998, he released the album "Leily Nahary", which saw tremendous success. He also performed concerts in the United States, Europe and Australia.

In 1999, he released the album "We Yeh" and won the Africa Music Award.

In 2000, he released the album "Tamally Ma'ak", which achieved massive sales globally and won him the World Music Award for the third time in the Arab world.

In 2001, he released the album "Banadeek Ta'ala", which garnered great popularity, especially the song "Banadeek Ta'ala" that achieved high viewership on YouTube.

In 2002, he launched the Amr Diab Academy to discover talents on YouTube. In November, he released two singles, "Waraiat" and "Aa'esh Ma'ak".

In 2003, he released the album "El Leila", which received immense acceptance from his fans.

In 2004, he released the album "Kammel Kalamak", which topped sales in the Middle East, including Egypt, Saudi Arabia, the UAE, Qatar and Lebanon.

In 2016, he released the album "Ahla W Ahla" and the album "Mn Asma Allah Al Hosna".

In 2017, he released the album "Maadi El Nas".
In 2018, he released the album "Kol Hayati".
In 2019, he released the album "Ana Gheir".
In 2020, he released the album "Sahran".

Richard Feynman

In an interview conducted with the physicist and Nobel laureate Richard Feynman, he told the interviewer about an approach that contributed to his exceptional physics achievements in the last century. He said: "To be able to accomplish significant physics work, you need a prolonged and absolute focus... Working in physics requires a lot of concentration... If you have a job, administrative tasks or anything of the sort, you won't have enough time for accomplishment. So, I invented a reputation for myself: I'm an irresponsible person. In fact, I'm effectively irresponsible. I've become the sort of person who tells everyone, 'I don't do anything'. And if someone asks me to be on a committee, I respond, 'No', and then I tell them afterward, 'I'm irresponsible'."

Feynman was determined to avoid administrative duties because he knew they would only diminish his ability to do the most important thing in his professional life: "To do great real physics work". As Cal Newport says, "We can recognize that Feynman would be a bad email responder and we can claim that he would have attempted to move from his university to another if the university administration required him to undertake numerous administrative tasks or forced him to tweet continuously. His clear understanding of what he wanted from his work led him to a clear understanding of what he also didn't want."

Neal Stephenson

If you visit the website of the renowned novelist and author of the most iconic books Neal Stephenson, you won't find his email address listed. A visitor to his site might understand the writer's intention through an article (https://www.nealstephenson.com) where he discusses his reluctance to display his email address, under the title "Why I'm Not a Good Correspondent".

The following are some key parts of this article:

"Authors who do not allow themselves to be constantly available to others are often labelled as 'uninterested'. While I do not consider myself 'uninterested', I have found it important to set certain boundaries on my communication with readers. These boundaries often morph into distractions that come in the form of emails or when, as I continuously accept invitations to become a speaker in various forums. This article adequately explains why I have chosen the approach of not constantly responding to others.

When I read a novel that I greatly admire, I feel a strong desire to directly communicate with its author. I sense a mental alignment and connection, and this might lead us to engage in stimulating discussions or even become friends if circumstances allow. When I'm nearing the end of a beautiful novel I'm reading, I feel a sense of disappointment. This feeling drives me to ensure a continued relationship with the author, a direct connection maintained through their other writings.

The novel represents years of hard work condensed into a few hundred pages, with all (or at least most) of the bad ideas that were discarded and cast aside before it, along with retaining the good ideas that were refined and reiterated as much as possible. The ideal interaction with the author is surpassed by nothing better than reading their novel.

The opportunity to meet an author face-to-face often ends without a full sense of satisfaction and the reader might even experience significant disappointment from such encounters.

Authors usually participate in gatherings that bring together a diverse group of intellectual figures, which is why it seems reasonable for them to occasionally take breaks from their creative writing for a few hours or days to attend events like conventions, book signings, workshops and the like. Here, ideas are meant to be exchanged with other authors and the broader community. As such, authors like me frequently receive invitations to such events.

Letters and emails from readers, including invitations to be an official speaker, could appear to be as something divergent from the norms of what writers do but in fact these events connect points and are quite common.

Email messages from readers and invitations to attend or speak at conferences, regardless of whether they're polite and rational requests (which they are in most cases), encourage authors to interact directly with their audience. However, for some authors, this process is straightforward and fitting, while for others, like myself, it is not.

There may be little or "nothing" I can offer my readers instead of what I have presented in my published writings. As a result, I make every effort to write more publishable pieces, rather than spend a few minutes here and a day there responding to emails or attending conferences.

Writing novels is a difficult task. It requires long and uninterrupted stretches of time. Four quiet hours are usually what I need to make progress. I might divide my time into two-hour slots during the day, but these are not as productive as the uninterrupted four hours. If I know something will interrupt, I can't focus, and if something will interrupt, I stop and can't do anything at all.

With this example, I can complete a substantial portion of the next book over several consecutive days, with four-hour time blocks. However, if those same hours are spread across a few weeks with interruptions in between, the result is almost non-productive.

The equation of productivity is not a straight and known line. By that, I mean this is why I say, "Why I'm not good at engaging and corresponding with people," and why I rarely accept general invitations or events of this kind. If I commit to organizing my life in the way I have found works for me, I get long, uninterrupted periods of time that allow me to write novels. But constant distractions and interruptions of this magnitude will substantially hinder my output as a novelist. The question is, what will replace this wasted time instead of a novel that will be around for long periods?

And if I'm lucky, many people will read it.

I've sent a large number of email messages to individuals, and a few of the lectures I've given at various events. I don't say the outcomes were bad but there was nothing I can call magnificent in any of them. So, for me, I've decided to choose one of two things: I can publish writings of moderate to medium quality to a small number of people, or I can publish higher quality material to a larger audience but I can't do both simultaneously. The former might overshadow the effort of the latter.

Another factor that led me to this choice is that writing fiction every day seems like a good way to maintain my mental health. If I were to tire myself with fiction writing, it could lead to agitation and become a source of distress for those around me. As long as I continue to write, being somewhat suitable for interacting with those around me, I've found that all the incentives point toward dedicating all available hours to writing fiction. I'm not truly proud that some of my emails might go unanswered as a result. It's never my intention to be rude or give the impression that I'm a cold or indifferent person.

If I were the most successful author, I would have enough money to hire staff to manage my emails. In reality, my books are purchased by enough people who provide me with a middle-class lifestyle but not enough to employ staff. Therefore, I face a difficult choice between being a poor correspondent and being a good novelist. In truth, I'm striving to be a good novelist and hope people will forgive my poor correspondence."

What Stephenson discusses in his article might seem "radical" in the lifestyle he has chosen for himself, which is to distance himself from the illusion of accomplishment in pursuit of true purpose. However, he fully grasped that maintaining long, uninterrupted periods of deep work is what might lead him to the journey to which he wants to dedicate his life. Note that he touches on the financial challenges that prevent him from employing others to respond to fan emails, yet at the same time, he recognizes that leaving an impact, encapsulated in the phrase "novels endure over long stretches, and if you're lucky, many people will read them," encourages him to engage in extended, uninterrupted focus, thus steering clear of what he believes some others might perceive as frequent appearances without true value to himself and others.

I'm not advocating this alarming level of disengagement from regular life but I always try, through stories and bold examples like these, to consider the extremes in the equation. The reverse situation to Stevenson's might be: an author with little output yet a constant presence at all official events, driven not necessarily by being important or sought after but as a necessity to fill an empty slot for event organizers. Thus, they don't necessarily seek a specific individual's presence for their value, but rather as a requirement to fill a slot.

Balance, in my opinion, is necessary, and most importantly is the safeguarding of those deep work periods for prolonged periods. This is to prevent "the talk" from defeating the depth of one's work, as Ryan Holiday mentioned.

Finale

In 2005, I bought a luxury jeans and t-shirt set from a renowned brand for the hefty price of 1,250 riyals. This sum amounted to a month's salary from my part-time job at a fast-food restaurant. This money was spent in less than half an hour.

The purchase was driven by a desire to prove to myself and to some of my friends that I could be like them, wearing fancy clothes and attending the same events as they did. It was an indirect attempt to seek appreciation, respect and recognition.

The occasion for this purchase was an invitation from a friend to visit "Durrat Al Arous" (a touristic village 23 kilometres from Jeddah) during that year's Eid Al Adha celebrations. Coinciding with the invitation, I received a call from my direct manager, urging me to start working at their branch in "Durrat Al Arous" during the holidays, promising a respectable salary increase. Regrettably, I declined the offer and refused to work there.

He persisted in his request, emphasizing the need for my presence at that branch, while I continued to refuse, citing that it was Eid and I didn't want to serve my friends from behind the counter instead of being with them.

As expected, I got fired for that reason. I sacrificed my job when my colleagues and managers needed me the most.

My income stopped and I faced arguments with my family when I asked them for money to manage my life after spending an entire month's salary on clothes that would not make any difference in my life and wouldn't impress anyone (I was still in my early twenties). Their problem was with the principle of it. How could I waste a month of hard work on buying clothes that others might or might not appreciate? And I ask myself today, was it the right decision to leave my job when they desperately needed me?

And I say: definitely not.

Today, as I write honestly about this technical mistake in my life, I genuinely hope readers (especially recent graduates) will realize that focusing on their own future and working on what gives real value to themselves before others is what will lead to positive results, not expensive clothes or presenting any image that tries to prove to others that they deserve respect. Even if my mistakes come back to me, I would prefer to invest that amount in buying books or shares in the parent company I used to work for. And certainly, I would have accepted the assignment to work at "Durrat Al Arous" during Eid.

Like many other people, I am still struggling with myself, torn between focusing on real work and deep work, while trying to avoid the illusion of achievement. The reason behind writing this book, with a focus on spending many hours on deep psychological and historical research about the concept of deep work and social status, is that I am genuinely struggling with this issue.

I wanted to know the reasons that subconsciously drive us to seek social status, even if it is far from reaching it. I wanted to explore the motivation behind many posts on social media channels, which I suddenly realized do not offer any real value, but rather a sense of achievement or an attempt to boost the ego. Before that, I wanted to find out the truth that shocked me when I met some people whose appearance in photos concealed significant flaws. I asked myself: Do others believe that I am covering my flaws with many photos? And does what I do every day lead me towards achieving what I want, or is it merely an attempt to tell others that I am just an amazing person?

Avoiding the "illusion of achievement" and distancing oneself from the "false social status" remains theoretically easy but challenging in reality. However, I have tried and continue to strive to apply every word written in this book to my daily life. My fear is that one day, someone noble may come and tell me, as mentioned in the Quran, "Do you order righteousness of the people and forget yourselves while you recite the Scripture?"[10] But I console myself again that this book was initially written as a reminder to myself first, and afterwards, to share it with others.

It is worth mentioning that I went through amusing situations during my research and work on this book. My life was turned upside down in some aspects, and I was greatly affected by the research findings and the quotes I shared in the previous pages. It led me to dispose of many of my possessions, and now I find myself pausing at every moment when I present something publicly, asking myself, "Is what I am doing an 'illusion of achievement', an attempt to boost my ego, or merely a pursuit of social status, or is it an action of real value?"

I feared I might become obsessed with these thoughts, so I decided to handle things calmly and appropriately. Another

---

10   Surat Al-Baqarah, verse 44

decision was to minimize what could be reduced in my life, hoping that now it may have a positive impact.

At that young age and with limited awareness, I applied everything criticized in this book. It was like seeking validation from others and avoiding real work, without recalling the unnecessary television appearance in 2009, which, from my current perspective, I see no reason for. But I remember at another time when I took a photo of myself during one of the television interviews and posted it on Facebook, tagging many friends on it. I thanked them for making my funny dream of appearing on television come true, to tell the public that I am important or to let them know that I am exceptional. Now, I talk about my company and my work.

What I didn't comprehend then that is clear to me now is that being in the limelight does not need to be the dream, it could be leaving an impact, like working on myself, my future and my daughters' future to positively influence them and those around me to change for the better before anything else. None of them will have their lives changed if I tell them that I took a picture with Michael Jackson[11] or appeared on a certain channel. Therefore, I won't completely stop these things to avoid criticism but I will focus on more productive work that serves and does not harm, without giving in to the illusion of achievement.

I hope we all stop before sharing anything or making any

---

11   I consider myself one of the biggest fans of the late singer Michael Jackson, and I read the excellent book "Michael Jackson, Inc." by Zack O'Malley. I summarized one of the most significant lessons I learned from his life in an article titled "What Makes a Person Less Intelligent as They Become Wealthier? The Story of Michael Jackson" on my blog, you can find article in the following link: /https://amoshrif.com/2017/03/mj

FINALE

purchase and ask ourselves: Will this increase the value of my achievements? Will it add value to others? Or is it merely an attempt to distract them? Do I want to feel important through this action or thing? When the appropriate answer comes, I will continue with what I intended to do.

I find that this book is an indirect continuation of my first book "The Art Revolution: How the artist works and how do others work". It is my hope from the bottom of my heart that you reach these pages, and that you give me a second chance to read my writings.

With all that being said, I wish the reader all the blessings, and more deep work, and more distance from the illusion of achievement.

Ahmed

Selected Readings & Bibliography

For some reason, many young Arab writers do not seem keen on citing sources or sharing their reading choices when researching topics for their books. However, I learned something valuable during my readings that I'd like to share. Whenever I read a book that intrigues me, I make sure to explore the references mentioned in it. Here, I'll list the most important references I used while creating the content of this book, hoping that readers might find interest in delving deeper into any of these topics.

I don't want to inconvenience readers who prefer not to explore foreign books or publications in their readings (though I must mention that most of my sources and research were based on publications written in English). I have tried to convey what I have learned in English into Arabic through my writings and articles on my page www.amoshrif.com.

Below are the most important books I consulted in my research for the content of this book:
De Botton, A. (2004). *Status Anxiety (Vintage International)* [Kindle Edition].
Le Bon, G. (2008). *Psychology of Crowds* [Kindle Edition].
Le Bon, G. (2008). *The Crowd: A Study of the Popular Mind* [Kindle Edition].
Barker, E. (2017). *Barking up the Wrong Tree: The*

Surprising Science Behind Why Everything You Know About Success Is (Mostly) Wrong.

Ericsson, A., & Pool, R. (2016). Peak: Secrets from the New Science of Expertise [Kindle Edition].

Newport, C. (2016). Deep Work: Rules for Focused Success in a Distracted World [Kindle Edition].

Holiday, R. (2017). Perennial Seller: The Art of Making and Marketing Work that Lasts [Paperback].

Manson, M. (2016). The Subtle Art of Not Giving a F*ck: A Counterintuitive Approach to Living a Good Life [Kindle Edition].

Peck, M. S. (2008). The Road Less Traveled: A New Psychology of Love, Traditional Values and Spiritual Growth [Kindle Edition].

Notes & References

1. Patel, N. (2014). The Psychology of Instant Gratification and How It Will Revolutionize Your Marketing Approach. Entrepreneur. Retrieved from [URL].
2. Heshmat, S. (2017). 10 Reasons We Rush for Immediate Gratification. Psychology Today. Retrieved from [URL].
3. Peck, M. S. (Year). The Road Less Traveled: A New Psychology of Love, Traditional Values and Spiritual Growth (pp. 31-32). Touchstone. Kindle Edition.
4. Ibid. (p. 15).
5. Ibid. (p. 16, 17).
6. Ibid. (p. 18).
7. Ibid. (p. 50).
8. Urban, T. (2017). Why Procrastinators Procrastinate - Wait But Why. Wait But Why. Retrieved from [URL].
9. Urban, T. (2017). Inside the Mind of a Master Procrastinator. TED. Retrieved from [URL].
10. Mischel, W., Shoda, Y., & Rodriguzez, M. L. (1989). Delay of gratification in children. Science, 244, 933-938.
11. Miller, D. T., & Karniol, R. (1976). The role of rewards in externally and self-imposed delay of gratification. Journal of Personality and Social Psychology, 33(5), 594-600.
12. De Botton, A. (Year). Status Anxiety (Vintage International) (Kindle Locations 142-144). Knopf Doubleday Publishing Group. Kindle Edition.

13. Le Bon, G. (1896). P. 54.
14. Le Bon, G. (1960). Psychologie des foules. Penguin (Non-Classics).
15. De Botton, A. (2017). A kinder, gentler philosophy of success. TED. Retrieved from [URL].
16. De Botton, A. (Year). Status Anxiety (Vintage International) (Kindle Locations 469-473). Knopf Doubleday Publishing Group. Kindle Edition.
17. Ibid. (Kindle Locations 474-477).
18. Ibid. (Kindle Locations 484-485).
19. Ibid. (Kindle Locations 107-108).
20. Ibid. (Kindle Locations 132-136).
21. De Botton, A. (Year). Status Anxiety (Vintage International) (Kindle Locations 274-275). Knopf Doubleday Publishing Group. Kindle Edition.
22. Ibid. (Kindle Locations 275-280).
23. Ibid. (Kindle Locations 649-653).
24. Ibid. (Kindle Locations 653-661).
25. Ibid. (Kindle Locations 663-671).
26. Ibid. (Kindle Locations 671-674).
27. Ibid. (Kindle Locations 719-725).
28. Ibid. (Kindle Locations 734-737).
29. Ibid. (Kindle Locations 745-751).
30. Donebyforty.com. (2018). Your Purchases Can't Buy You Class. Retrieved from [URL].
31. Ravenscraft, E. (2018). Don't Try to Buy Your Way to Status, Earn It Instead. Lifehacker. Retrieved from [URL].
32. De Botton, A. (Year). Status Anxiety (Vintage International) (Kindle Locations 137-139). Knopf Doubleday Publishing Group. Kindle Edition.

33. Manson, M. (Year). The Subtle Art of Not Giving a Fck: A Counterintuitive Approach to Living a Good Life* (pp. 3-4). HarperCollins. Retrieved from [URL].
34. Manson, M. (Year). The Subtle Art of Not Giving a Fck: A Counterintuitive Approach to Living a Good Life* (p. 80). HarperCollins. Retrieved from [URL].
35. Le Bon, G. (Year). Psychology of Crowds (Kindle Locations 74-78). Sparkling Books Limited. Kindle Edition.
36. Ibid. (Kindle Locations 272-282).
37. Ibid. (Kindle Locations 297-300).
38. Newport, C. (2016). Deep Work: Rules for Focused Success in a Distracted World (1st ed.). Grand Central Publishing.
39. Currey, M. (2013). Daily Rituals: How Artists Work (1st ed.). Knopf.
40. Newport, C. (2016). Deep Work: Rules for Focused Success in a Distracted World (1st ed.). Grand Central Publishing, p. 2.
41. Ibid. p. 2.
42. Various. (2015). 100 Events That Changed the World (National Geographic Magazine). Wall Periodicals Online, p. 71.
43. Goins, J. (2017). Real Artists Don't Starve: Timeless Strategies for Thriving in the New Creative Age. Thomas Nelson.
44. Ward, M. (2017). Warren Buffett's reading routine could make you smarter, science suggests. CNBC. Retrieved from [URL].
45. Newport, C. (2016). Deep Work: Rules for Focused Success in a Distracted World (1st ed.). Grand Central

Publishing, p. 3.
46. Ibid. p. 3.
47. Newport, C. (2016). Deep Work: Rules for Focused Success in a Distracted World (1st ed.). Grand Central Publishing, p. 4.
48. Newport, C. (2018). Woody Allen and the Art of Value Productivity—Study Hacks - Cal Newport. Retrieved from [URL].
49. Ibid.
50. Ericsson, A., & Pool, R. (2017). Peak: Secrets from the New Science of Expertise (Reprint ed.). Eamon Dolan/Mariner Books.
51. Ericsson, A., Krampe, R. T., & Tesch-Romer, C. (1993). The Role of Deliberate Practice in the Acquisition of Expert Performance. Psychological Review, 100(3), 363-406.
52. Barker, E. (2017). Barking Up the Wrong Tree: The Surprising Science Behind Why Everything You Know About Success Is (Mostly) Wrong. HarperOne.
53. Holiday, R. (2017). Perennial Seller: The Art of Making and Marketing Work that Lasts. Portfolio, p. 27.
54. Newport, C. (2018). Monday Master Class: Don't Use a Daily To-Do List—Study Hacks - Cal Newport. Retrieved from [URL].
55. Kimmel Live, J. (2018). Tom Ford Has Many Talents [Video]. YouTube. Retrieved from [URL].
56. Holiday, R. (2017). Perennial Seller: The Art of Making and Marketing Work that Lasts. Portfolio, p. 21.
57. Newport, C. (2016). Deep Work: Rules for Focused Success in a Distracted World (1st ed.). Grand Central Publishing, p. 62.